W9-AIM-705

33 THE SERIES™

AUTHENTIC MANHOOD™

VOLUME **1** TRAINING GUIDE

A **MAN** AND HIS **DESIGN**

authenticmanhood.com

A **MAN** AND HIS **DESIGN**

Published by Authentic Manhood • Copyright 2012 Fellowship Associates Inc. • Reprinted 2019

No part of this book may be reproduced or transmitted in any form or by any means, electronic or mechanical, including photocopying and recording, or by any information storage or retrieval system, except as may be expressly permitted in writing by the publisher. Requests to duplicate any aspect of this training guide should be addressed in writing to Authentic Manhood; 12115 Hinson Road, Suite 200; Little Rock, AR 72212; 501-975-5050.

Project Management: Grant Guffin, Flashlight Media Group, LLC
Art Direction and Design: Mike Robinson, Details Communications
Editors: Rick Caldwell, Grant Guffin, Brian Jones, Rachel Lindholm, Steve Snider, Rebekah Wallace, Lindsey Woodward
Contributing Writers: John Bryson, Rick Caldwell, Bryan Carter, Grant Edwards, Tierce Green, Grant Guffin,
    Jeff D. Lawrence, Traylor Lovvorn, Steve Snider

In association with Flashlight Media Group, LLC; 3860 Forest Hill Irene Road, Suite 106; Memphis, TN 38125; 901-755-1011; www.flashlightmediagroup.com

Authentic Manhood, Men's Fraternity and 33 The Series are registered trademarks of Fellowship Associates Inc.

To order additional copies of this resource, go to AuthenticManhood.com or LifeWay.com.

Printed in the United States of America

Distributed by:

Authentic Manhood
12115 Hinson Road, Suite 200
Little Rock, AR 72212

Groups Ministry Publishing
LifeWay Resources
One LifeWay Plaza
Nashville, TN 37234

TABLE of CONTENTS

The Importance of Being in a **Community of Men**

Climbing a mountain alone is a difficult and even dangerous idea. Attempting to climb the mountain of manhood alone is also not recommended. Just like a literal mountain climber needs to belay or connect with another man for safety and support, we need other men around us to help us stay on course with our manhood. *Having other guys deeply connected to us becomes invaluable when we slip, struggle, or stray off course in our manhood journey.*

One of the biggest mistakes you can make with regards to *33 The Series* is to watch or listen to this material in isolation. The goal of this study is not just to fill in the blanks of your **Training Guide,** but also to actually fill in the blanks of your life. Having other men walk through the experience with you is the key to moving this material from the pages of your **Training Guide** to actually being fleshed out in your everyday life.

MANHOOD COMMUNITY

1 Provides encouragement. Every man needs other men cheering for him and encouraging him on his journey to manhood.

2 Gives you additional insight. Having other men around you helps you get a much better perspective on your life. Others can help you discover your blind spots and avoid costly mistakes.

3 Brings constructive criticism. We all need men in our lives who will be honest with us to help us become better men.

4 Makes your journey richer. Sharing life with a community of men makes the great times feel like a celebration and provides much needed support when life gets rough.

No one can force you to open up your life and work to make a connection with another man. Although it can be challenging and frightening, it's well worth the risk. **33**

From a **Weekly Gathering** to a **Global Movement**

Several years ago, Dr. Robert Lewis responded to the desire of a handful of men who were hungering for more than a Bible study. They wanted a map for manhood – a definition of what it meant to be a man. They needed help to leap over the hurdles they were encountering in life and they needed healing from the wounds of their past.

Robert responded by launching a weekly gathering called Men's Fraternity, challenging men to join him at six o'clock each Wednesday morning for twenty-four weeks. From the depth of his own personal experience and the pages of Scripture, Robert developed what came to be known as the Men's Fraternity series:

- *The Quest for Authentic Manhood*
- *Winning at Work & Home*
- *The Great Adventure*

What began with a few men huddling up to talk about what it meant to be a man rapidly grew into a weekly gathering of more than three hundred men. In just a few years, local attendance at Men's Fraternity climbed to more than one thousand men.

The message of Authentic Manhood that began at Men's Fraternity could not be contained in that room. It began to spread and soon exploded into a global movement *impacting more than a million men in more than 20,000 locations worldwide* – from locker rooms to boardrooms, from churches to prisons, on military bases and the field of battle, at NASA and even on a space shuttle mission. Wherever the messages were heard, the challenge has remained the same. It is the call for men to step up and follow the biblical manhood modeled by Jesus Christ.

The Men's Fraternity curriculum was not developed in a corporate cubicle environment, written by an out-of-touch writer and pushed on men as a nice thing to do. *It was created on the front lines where men live, written in the trenches in response to men who pleaded for purpose and direction.* It

has proven to be the most widely used and effective material on Authentic Manhood available today. *What began as a weekly meeting of men searching for answers to their manhood questions has grown into a bold movement that has dramatically impacted the lives of men, their families and communities.* 33

Presenter Profiles

JOHN BRYSON

Seeing firsthand the impact the original Men's Fraternity curriculum had on his own life, John Bryson decided to teach the material himself. In the years since, he's led thousands of men through the basic ideas of biblical manhood. Most recently, he's launched groups for men in 20 different cities and college campuses.

John is a co-founding teaching pastor of Fellowship Memphis, a multi-cultural church ministering in the evolving urban core of Memphis, Tennessee.

In 2010, he completed his Doctor of Ministry in "Redemptive and Organizational Leadership" from Gordon-Conwell Theological Seminary. John is also the author of *College Ready,* a curriculum for college students, and travels the country consulting and investing in churches, church planters, leaders and new ideas.

A native of Harlan, Kentucky, John played baseball at Asbury College.

He and his wife Beth have 5 kids: Brooke, Beck, Bo, Boss and Blair.

BRYAN CARTER

Bryan Carter taught the original Men's Fraternity curriculum to a group of more than 800 men over a three-year period at Concord Church. Additionally, he's been a frequent speaker at local and international churches, conferences and events.

Bryan is the Senior Pastor of Concord Church in Dallas, Texas.

He is author of a 28-day devotional book entitled, *Great Expectations.* Bryan also contributed to the book *What Two White Men of God Learned from Black Men of God,* co-authored by Dr. Joel Gregory and Dr. Bill Crouch.

A recreational basketball player, Bryan is a fan of the NBA's Dallas Mavericks.

Bryan and his wife Stephanie are the parents of two daughters, Kaitlyn and Kennedy, and one son, Carson.

TIERCE GREEN

Tierce Green teaches the principles of Authentic Manhood to well over a thousand men each week at a gathering called *The Quest.* He is also one of the teaching pastors in the bullpen for his Senior Pastor, Kerry Shook.

Tierce is the Executive Pastor of Small Groups at Woodlands Church in The Woodlands, Texas.

Prior to joining the staff at Woodlands Church, Tierce was a speaker and consultant for conferences, retreats and churches across the country for twenty-six years. He has written curriculum for Student Life, North American Mission Board and LifeWay. His most recent project is a 12-week series for men called *Fight Club: Some Things Are Worth Fighting For.*

A lifelong Dallas Cowboys fan, Tierce's favorite activities include landscaping, good food and conversation.

He and his wife Dana have one daughter, Anna.

Manhood Realities

SESSION **ONE** | Training Guide **NOTES**

Manhood Realities

I. INTRODUCTION

Our world desperately needs better _____.

II. CURRENT MANHOOD REALITIES

1. Men are in a state of _____.

2. Men are experiencing a general disappointment with life.

3. Men are experiencing _____.

4. Men are lonely.

5. Men are _____.

6. Men are turning to escapes to numb the pain.

7. Confused men create major _____. For example:

• Recent statistics reveal that 90% of murders are committed by men. 88% of robberies are committed by men,[1] and 75% of all people arrested are men.[2]

• "Gender is the single best predictor of criminal behavior: men commit more crime, and women commit less. This distinction holds throughout history, for all societies, for all groups, and for nearly every crime category."[3]

8. Without a compelling _____ for manhood, men will settle for less in life.

[1] U.S. Department of Justice, "Crime in the United States." Table 42. Online: http://www2.fbi.gov/ucr/cius2009/data/table_42.html.
[2] U.S. Department of Justice, "Crime in the United States." Overview. Online: http://www2.fbi.gov/ucr/cius2009/arrests/index.html.
[3] Darrell Steffensmeier and Emilie Allan, "Gender and Crime," in Encyclopedia of Crime and Justice, ed. Joshua Dressler (Macmillan Reference, 2002), 728.

III. HISTORICAL ROOTS OF OUR PRESENT MANHOOD CRISIS

1. Racism

2. The Industrial Revolution

3. The War Years

4. Feminism

5. Extended Adolescence

IV. CONCLUSION

1. You need to show up.

2. You need a team.

3. Preview of future sessions.

DISCUSSION / REFLECTION QUESTIONS

1.   Why did you join this manhood journey? What expectations do you have personally?

2.   What stood out to you the most from session one?

3.   Are you experiencing any of the current "manhood realities" discussed?

4.   Have any of the historical roots of our current manhood crisis affected you, if so how?

SUPPORTING RESOURCES

Cross, Gary. *Men to Boys: The Making of Modern Immaturity.* Columbia University Press, 2008. A historian's explanation of extended adolescence.

Kimmel, Michael. *Guyland: The Perilous World Where Boys Become Men.* Harper Collins, 2009. A sociologist's perspective on extended adolescence.

Piper, John and Wayne Grudem, eds. *Recovering Biblical Manhood and Womanhood: A Response to Evangelical Feminism.* Crossway Books, 2006. A collection of articles by evangelical scholars countering the claims of evangelical feminism.

Rhoads, Steven E. *Taking Sex Differences Seriously.* Encounter Books, 2004. An analysis of the scientific evidence demonstrating that male and female role distinctions are based in biology and are not merely socially constructed.

Sommers, Christina Hoff. *The War Against Boys: How Misguided Feminism is Harming Our Young Men.* Simon and Schuster, 2001. Philosopher Christina Hoff Sommers discusses the negative effects of feminism on men.

Wise, Tim. *White Like Me: Reflections on Race from a Privileged Son.* Soft Skull Press, 2008. Reflections on the advantages and disadvantages of race from a prominent antiracist author.

The content in the supporting resources above does not necessarily reflect the opinion of Authentic Manhood. Not all of the books are written from a Christian perspective. Readers should use these books as resources but form their own opinions.

Recalculating By Bryan Carter

That's the word I see on my GPS when I miss a turn or go the wrong direction. **RECALCULATING.** Even when I feel like I'm on the right track, that one word—recalculating—gives me a vivid reminder that I need to make immediate adjustments if I'm going to reach my destination.

In many ways, Session One is like pausing to recalculate where we are as men on our journey to manhood. The great reality of life is that even with the best of intentions, every man will make a wrong turn at some point. Yet, when you make that wrong turn, one of the keys to your Authentic Manhood journey is not to focus too much on the mistaken turn, but to make proper adjustments for the future.

SOME MEN CHOOSE TO TURN ONTO BOYHOOD BOULEVARD.

Boyhood. Those were exceptional days. We played all day, hung out with our friends, did only the things that made us happy, had no responsibility or accountability... the good 'ol days of growing up. The reality of boyhood is that it is intended to be an on-ramp to responsibility not a boulevard to continuous cruising. **It's time to RECALCULATE.**

SOME MEN CHOOSE TO TURN ONTO CAREER COURT.

Our careers are important and work is part of God's divine design for our lives, yet there is much more to life than work. Most of us get an incredible rush from a job well done or from success accomplished in the workplace. We are performers by nature and we thrive in these environments. We work long hours, take on additional responsibilities, but often we do it at the expense of our families and our own personal lives. **It's time to RECALCULATE.**

SOME MEN CHOOSE TO TURN ONTO APPETITE AVENUE.

Appetites are inner desires we all possess. They are healthy and designed for our own growth and development. We have appetites for food, success, sex, love and other things. Yet when these appetites go unchecked, they can cause considerable damage in our lives. When a man turns onto this road and allows his appetites to control his life,

"No matter where you may have made a wrong turn, this is your opportunity to make the course correction toward a better life."

 # NEXT STEPS...

YOU'VE RECALCULATED. Maybe, you're headed down some wrong paths. You want to make a change—take steps toward becoming the man you were made to be, the man you've dreamed you could be—but you don't know how to begin. Consider these simple, but effective, steps:

1 **TRUST AND PRAY |** Ask God for strength to embrace a new life. Trust Him to do what you're unable to do on your own.

2 **THINK |** If you're given 80 years on this Earth, what's the best use of the time you have remaining? What do you want your story and your legacy to be?

3 **SPEAK UP |** Take a close friend, a pastor, or a trusted advisor to lunch and come clean. Saying the words out loud to someone you trust is a big step away from destructive behavior and toward a new life.

4 **CHANGE YOUR COURSE |** If you're engaged in destructive behavior, step away from it. Remove yourself from the source of your temptation and replace destructive behavior with healthy behavior.

5 **FIND A MENTOR |** There are men who have already walked the path you're considering. Seek them out—we can't do this journey alone.

6 **SEEK COUNSELING OR A SUPPORT GROUP |** Some behaviors are difficult to break, and years of destructive living have come with potentially far-reaching consequences. Spending time with a Christian counselor or a support group is a wise move for those dealing with excess baggage.

he's headed straight for disaster. **It's time to RECALCULATE.**

No matter where you may have made a wrong turn, this is your opportunity to make the course corrections toward a better life, toward the full life that God says is available to all of us. The simple fact that you've already begun to explore this material on Authentic Manhood reveals that you have the steering wheel in your hand and you've chosen to head down the path toward a life of Authentic Manhood, the life that brings true joy and fulfillment. If you're not dead, you're not done. Welcome to the journey!

It's time to RECALCULATE. 🔗

colla
damage

I can be in Birmingham tonight

[IF YOU WANT ME TO BE.]

By Traylor Lovvorn

teral

IT WAS A BRISK SATURDAY MORNING in early fall when those words popped up in a chat window on my computer screen.

MELODY, MY WIFE, was at the grocery store and I was home alone, having just logged into an online instant messenger service I used often. The woman on the other end of that post lived somewhere in Kentucky. I had recently made contact with her in an online chat room.

An adult chat room. I stared at the words on my screen. My heartbeat sped up...palms began to sweat.

 How easy it would have been to simply ignore her post. How easy it would have been to tell her that I was not available to meet her later.

It was the moment of decision. I had recently found myself in adult chat rooms again after a ten-month hiatus. I started back innocently enough with sports chat, but quickly migrated back to the seedy and titillating adult rooms full of other bored, lonely, checked-out people looking to connect with someone...anyone. Chat rooms and pornography gave me an instant escape from the pain of my past and the uncertainty of my present.

And there I sat staring at those haunting words on my screen...watching the cursor blink...knowing she was on the other end waiting for a response.

I typed, "Ok" and, after what seemed like forever, finally hit "send."

At that moment, I knew my life would never be the same. Paralyzing fear and intense excitement rushed through me simultaneously. Terrifying fear because I knew what she was coming for and I knew that I would cross that final line...if for no other reason than because she had driven all the way from Kentucky and I felt some twisted sense of obligation. The excitement flowed from playing with the forbidden. A needy and desperate part of me relished the fact that someone... anyone... was willing to drive over 350 miles to meet me.

I had sex with her that night and never even got her last name. Today, I can't even remember her first name. I never spoke to her again, but the damage had been done. I had added physical adultery to my secret life of pornography and chat rooms. I crossed a line that I never imagined crossing. The lies I had fed myself for years about pornography being innocent and "something men do" mocked me as I drove home that fateful Saturday night.

One word consumed my thoughts. Adulterer.

One word consumed my thoughts. Adulterer. The shame I felt and the contempt I had for myself was suffocating. I didn't recognize who I had become. What I had convinced myself was "not a big deal" had literally sucked the life out of me. I had become a shell of a man thinking only about the next opportunity I would have alone in order to get my fix.

And then I thought about my wife and kids. Telling Melody what I had done was not even remotely on my radar. I vowed this was the last time and was successful in "white-knuckling" my way around it for a while. Nine months later it happened again.

And again. And again. And again. By the time my secrets came out, it had happened seven times. Seven times over a three-year period. Secrets. Lies. Cover-up.

I was a desperate, conflicted, empty shell. I was a confused man...creating major problems. And then my two worlds collided and I was exposed. It was a beautiful undoing. Pain and relief rushed into my empty soul simultaneously.

I finally stepped off my performance treadmill and was slapped in the face with the utter devastation my selfish behavior had caused. Words can't describe my wife's heartache and anguish over years of deception and betrayal. Her anguishing wail from behind our locked bedroom door will forever haunt me.

Our divorce was final in December of 2002.

I was panicked and dejecte

recovery:
The journey home

My secret struggle devastated my wife and four precious children. It had also devastated me and led me to places I never dreamed I would go. It took losing my wife and kids for me to wake up and, like the prodigal son in Luke 15 who finally hit rock bottom and wandered back home, decide to come home. Unfortunately, I had drifted blindly for so many years that I first had to figure out where I was and how I had gotten there. Like the proverbial frog who failed to recognize the gradual changes in the water's temperature, I had been cooked alive.

The watershed event that threw me into the pot, so to speak, happened in the fall of 1993 when I was 22 years old. Though I had been exposed to pornography when I was 8, everything in my life had basically unfolded in a positive direction until then. I considered myself on the path of spiritual maturity as a teenager. I was able to keep my porn habit as an occasional, secret place of escape. My ultimate dreams were to play Division 1 basketball and become a pastor, leading others on their spiritual journeys.

During my junior year in high school, Samford University, a school that had just moved to Division 1, started recruiting me. They later had a change of heart and stopped recruiting me for an athletic scholarship, but instead asked me to be an invited walk-on. By that time I had secured a Presidential scholarship to Samford, so I still felt like everything was on track. I could clearly see how God was working things out.

Soon after arriving on campus, I realized I didn't have a spot on the team. I was devastated. My dream to play Division 1 basketball was crushed and it hurt deeply. Then, a few weeks later I got a call inviting me to pastor a new church plant starting nearby. One door closed and another opened, leaving me to reason that God had closed the door to my basketball dream so that I could fully devote my energies to becoming a pastor. This experience would set me up perfectly to make the most of future opportunities.

When graduation arrived in May 1993, I resigned from the church plant. Almost immediately, the perfect job seemed to present itself. I would travel the country, sharpening my skills as a communicator and leader, while making a difference in the lives of others. Things were coming together. It was all working out perfectly.

Then, out of nowhere, that door slammed shut. I was panicked and dejected. The next week, I found myself answering want ads, hoping to find a job so I could squeak out a living. I finally found a job in sales—something I'd never pictured myself doing. I had a dream, a quality education, solid experience and no doors to walk through. Selling cell phones in Birmingham wasn't a part of my plan. Couldn't be. As a result, I came to two fatal conclusions about God and His heart toward me based on that series of events:

| **1** | God is angry about my struggle with pornography and this is His punishment. | **2** | God can't be counted on to take care of me. I am on my own. |

Those two deadly lies began a slow drift that carried me aimlessly to that fateful Saturday morning staring at the blinking cursor of my computer. It wasn't a conscious parting of ways, but deep inside I felt like God was mad at me, punishing me, and that I had better fix things on my own so I could once again have fellowship with Him. I dutifully vowed to work harder and be more devout, but in my heart I wasn't so sure God could  be trusted. I developed a strong sense that I was an orphan, on my own with a huge, perceived rift between God and me.

For the next decade, I dutifully went through the motions of being a devoted Christian husband and father, vowing over and

...d a dream, a quality education, solid experience and no doors to walk through.

I also discovered that God really does love me unconditionally and I don't have to hide who I really am.

over to "turn over a new leaf" and be more disciplined. I successfully walled myself off emotionally from those closest to me in order to avoid the possibility of being hurt any further. I numbed the ache of my soul by escaping to adult chat rooms...preferring to live in a virtual world that didn't exist because I was too much of a coward to allow myself to live in the real world.

But early one morning as I was reading the Bible, God's grace broke through with this thought:

"God knew all about my sexual addiction and seven affairs when He saved me at the age of 11."

That lone thought broke the logjam of unbelief in my mind and I began to understand just how amazing and wonderful God's grace is. I began to uncover more lies I had bought into that further skewed my view of God and His tender mercies toward me. I realized I had related to God in two inconsistent ways at the same time. I vacillated between believing God loved me because of my performance on the one hand, and thinking I had forfeited my relationship with my Father because of my habitual sin on the other.

My journey home has been painful and gut wrenching and there were many times I wondered if it was worth it. Along the way I discovered that true, genuine healing is found on the other side of pain. On this journey, God exposed my deep unbelief. And I discovered I could invite Him into my pain and trust that He desired to heal my brokenness.

I also discovered that God really does love me unconditionally and I don't have to hide who I really am. I no longer have to keep people at arm's length to protect my reputation. I can drop the masks that I hid behind for so long and connect with others at a point of weakness rather than trying to impress with strength. My own recovery journey into Authentic Manhood has taught me to live as God's beloved son instead of believing the lie that I'm an abandoned orphan who has to figure life out on his own.

The rest of the story

Melody and I were married for 11 years before my struggle with pornography and sexual addiction ripped our family apart. This tragic upheaval left both of us reeling and disrupted our status quo, to say the least. The appearance of the "perfect" life that we both worked so hard to maintain came crashing down around us in 2002.

I did not realize it at the time, but God placed us both on a journey into authenticity after our divorce. This journey painfully exposed the deep unbelief that haunted us and kept us on our performance treadmill for years. God lovingly brought us both to the end of ourselves and, after six years of divorce, we were remarried in October of 2008.

You can read more about our redemptive, grace story at our blog, **Ragamuffin Reflections**, at **ragamuffinreflections.com**. We also have a recovery ministry that offers help and hope to individuals and couples that have been impacted by porn and sex addiction called **Route1520 (route1520.com).**

God lovingly brought us both to the end of ourselves and, after six years of divorce, we were remarried in October of 2008.

Create and Cultivate

SESSION **TWO** | Training Guide **NOTES**

Create and Cultivate

I. INTRODUCTION[1]

1. The manhood realities discussed in session one should be a startling _____ call for all of us.

2. We want to bring **clarity** to our confusion about manhood.

II. THE ORIGINAL MANHOOD DESIGN: **CREATE AND CULTIVATE**

1. In chapter one of Genesis, we see God model _____ through two specific actions:

    •   God **creates**

    •   God **cultivates**

2. Genesis 1:27 "So God created man in his own image, in the image of God he created him." (ESV)

    God intended man to be like _____.

3. Genesis 1:28 "Be fruitful and multiply and fill the earth and subdue it and have dominion over the fish of the sea and over the birds of the heavens and over every living thing that moves on the earth." (ESV)

    •   God has given us a mandate to _____ and _____.

4. God created men to be **social** and **spiritual** leaders.

[1] The material in this session has been influenced by Timothy Keller, "The Prodigal God: Recovering the Heart of the Christian Faith" (Dutton, 2008); Andy Crouch, "Culture Making: Recovering Our Creative Calling" (Downers Grove: InterVarsity Press, 2008); Mark Driscoll, "The Birth of John the Baptizer." Online: http://www.marshillchurch.org/media/luke/the-birth-of-john-the-baptize

5. When men don't lead, _____ follows.

- Consider the disorder and confusion that occurs in a home when a father abandons his responsibility to raise his children.

- Statistically, children growing up in father-absent homes are far more likely to die in infancy, live in poverty, end up in prison, use drugs, be abused, or drop out of school.[2]

6. Masculinity is not about just being a _____ leader. It's about having the courage to just do it.

III. MISUNDERSTANDING GOD'S DESIGN

1. Adam **failed** in these areas. He did not show the courage to lead.

- Genesis 3:6 "So when the woman saw that the tree was good for food, and that it was a delight to the eyes ... she took of its fruit and ate, and she also gave some to her husband who was with her, and he ate." (ESV)

2. There are two typical "misses" when it comes to experiencing God's best for our life.[3]

1) The way of the _____ (Genesis 3:6)

- Adam and Eve chose their own way over God's **will**.

2) The way of the _____ (Genesis 3:7)

- Those who try to **cover** themselves with good behavior and try

to **perform** their way into God's favor.

[2] The National Fatherhood Initiative, "Data on the Consequences of Father Absence." Online: http://www.fatherhood.org/Page.aspx?pid=403
[3] For more information on the typical "misses" to experiencing God's best see Timothy Keller, The Prodigal God: Recovering the Heart of the Christian Faith (Dutton, 2008).

IV. GOD'S SOLUTION

1. God _____ for Adam and Eve despite their sin.

   • Genesis 3:21 "and the Lord God made for Adam and for his wife garments of skins and clothed them." (ESV)

2. God has made provision for us through his son, **Jesus**.

3. Jesus not only models an inspiring masculinity, He also **enables** us to live it ourselves.

4. Just like Adam and Eve, we are all _____.

5. Our sin is an **offense** to a perfect and holy God.

6. Here is the good news, God gives us grace through Jesus:

   • Romans 5:8 "God shows his love for us in that while we were still sinners, Christ died for us." (ESV)

   • Romans 3:22 "Righteousness from God comes through faith in Jesus Christ to all who believe." (ESV)

   • 1 Timothy 2:5 "There is one mediator between God and man, the man Christ Jesus." (ESV)

7. Only by placing our trust in Jesus can we have salvation as well as the
    _____ that fuels the Authentic Manhood we're talking about.

    ## To further explore trusting Jesus with your life, check out the online video at authenticmanhood.com.

V. MISUNDERSTANDING MANHOOD

The same misses of Adam and Eve, the fruit and the fig leaves, can show up in the "misses" of today's conventional manhood.[4]

1. Men who choose the way of the fruit become _____ consumers.

    •   They become totally obsessed with _____.

    •   1 Corinthians 15:45 tells us that our model, Jesus, is a **life-giving** spirit.

2. Men who choose the way of the fig leaves become _____ and _____.

    •   They take pride in what they _____ do.

    •   They would rather **criticize** than create.

3. Without a clear understanding of Authentic Manhood, we will all be tempted to be childish consumers or cowards and critics.

VI. CONCLUSION

1. How should we respond to God's mandate for us to create & cultivate?

    •   _____ Jesus for our salvation and look to Him as our model for Authentic Manhood.

    •   Embrace the mandate today:

        ○   Have courage to live it out at work according to how God has **wired** you

        ○   Be creative with your wife, cultivating that relationship by giving her something to anticipate

        ○   Be a _____ for your kids by leading them as you passionately follow God

2. This session was about the big picture of our manhood mandate. In the next session, we will explore a clear and compelling biblical definition of what it means to be a man.

DISCUSSION / REFLECTION QUESTIONS

1. How are you creating and cultivating in the different roles in your life? As a husband? As a father? At work? As a friend? Are you being a "life-giving spirit" (1 Corinthians 15:45)?

2. Are you more tempted to run away from God toward the pleasures of this world (the way of the fruit) or are you more likely to try to impress God with your accomplishments (the way of the fig leaves)?

3. What has God provided for us through Jesus?

4. Is it easier for you to be a consumer or a critic?

SUPPORTING RESOURCES

Crouch, Andy. *Culture Making: Recovering Our Creative Calling.* IVP Books, 2008. In this book author Andy Crouch argues that all Christians should be "creating" and "cultivating" culture.

Keller, Tim. *The Prodigal God: Recovering the Heart of the Christian Faith.* Dutton, 2008. Pastor Tim Keller uses the parable of the prodigal son to explain the Christian message. A great introduction to the heart of Christianity.

Phillips, Richard D. *The Masculine Mandate: God's Calling to Men.* Reformation Trust Publishing, 2010. A pastor's explanation of Genesis 1–3 as it relates to manhood. A nice complement to this session.

The content in the supporting resources above does not necessarily reflect the opinion of Authentic Manhood. Readers should use these books as resources but form their own opinions.

Living the Mandate By John Bryson

God has "hard-wired" men to create and cultivate. I believe at the core of a man's heart he must be creating and taking initiative for the benefit of others to feel a sense of significance, meaning, purpose and fulfillment. As we covered extensively in this session, God models creation and cultivation as early as Genesis 1 and 2, then mandates those two acts of courage to Adam as the core essence, responsibility and purpose of his masculinity. That mandate is still ours as men today.

That is why there is something that innately inspires us as men when we see an entrepreneur create a new business from scratch and use it to bless others; a new principal turn around a failing school; a father navigate his family through a tough season; or a coach create a winning culture for a team. When men step into responsibility, whether that's in their home, neighborhood, workplace or city, and create a situation that betters others, those men and all who see and experience their leadership are both inspired and left with a deep sense of what is good, noble and right.

> *It is sad and should be terrifying how easy it is for us as men to slip on the clothes of passivity, mediocrity and insignificance. Authentic Men reject all that.*

I wish you could all get to know and watch my friend David Montague create and cultivate. David stepped out of a successful career as a bond salesman to get on the solution side of a national pandemic, urban education in America. Over the last few years, David has pioneered and nurtured the Memphis Teacher Residency program that has recruited and clustered young, talented educators, given them elite training, and placed them into the most vulnerable schools in Memphis. He has been a man on a mission and the fruit of his efforts are incredible.

Stepping up and stepping out as a man to create or fix something or flesh out a vision that God has put on your heart often creates fertile soil for a man's inner life. God will often do more in you than through you when you step into Authentic Manhood. Kennan Vaughan discussed this with me when I asked him about Downline Ministries, a discipleship effort he began six years ago. I asked him first about the obstacles and challenges he faced in creating a new movement: *"I felt the overwhelming odds against success that would often lead to potential discouragement or hopelessness, that would then turn to frustration. That frustration always became a fork in the road for me, either it would nullify any redemptive efforts or it would fuel the flame to push forward."* I also asked Kennan to talk about some of the things that began to happen inside of him, at a soul level, as he pressed forward into the vision God had placed on his heart. Kennan said, "God increased my faith, humility, passion and prayer life." I asked Kennan what he has learned about himself, God and others on this adventure, "God is big and worth trusting. I am small and I must follow Him every step of the way. Others are often passive, so my steps of initiative benefit them. Finally, God seems to bless radical steps of obedience that bring Him glory!"

Just like Kennan, any man who has been beckoned off the sidelines and onto the front lines of any new initiative will talk about the challenges and obstacles. There are some land mines we must navigate as men in order to live out the create and cultivate mandate. One land mine for all men is *passivity.* It is dangerously easy for us as men to not act. Passivity feels more comfortable than initiative. Another land mine is a *lack of courage.* Like the cowardly Lion in the Wizard of Oz, many of us lack courage. *Cynicism* is also a barrier. Can we really make a difference anyway? Will any of this work? How about the inability to follow through for many of us. Great ideas that never see the light of day and stay stuck unfinished.

Finally, the familiar clothes of selfishness can distract us. Simply being consumed by self. Those are just a few of the character flaws that prevent a man from living up to his mandate and doing life at a high level. It is sad and should be terrifying how easy it is for us as men to slip on the clothes of passivity, mediocrity and insignificance. Authentic men reject all that. Let's "Man Up" and make create and cultivate our new normal in every phase and season of life. **33**

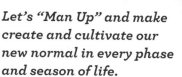

Let's "Man Up" and make create and cultivate our new normal in every phase and season of life.

BLAZING THE TRAIL

You may not be the next Steve Jobs or Thomas Edison, but you can learn a lot from observing the way others think, overcome obstacles and invest their time. Read the stories of these creators and cultivators as you're considering ways you can make an impact in your home, workplace, church and community.

1. ***Steve Jobs*** by Walter Isaacson- The author profiles the man who revolutionized the world of personal computing. Read about the creation of the first Apple computer as well as the invention of the iPod, iPad, iPhone and the launch of Pixar.

2. ***Fist Stick Knife Gun: A Personal History of Violence in America*** by Geoffrey Canada- The president and CEO of the Harlem Children's Zone presents a powerful portrayal of the challenges facing urban African American males and offers solutions as well.

3. ***Start Something That Matters*** by Blake Mycoskie- The founder of TOMS Shoes, a company that gives a pair of shoes away to economically disadvantaged people for each pair of shoes purchased, outlines a simple philosophy for making a difference.

4. ***Gifted Hands: The Ben Carson Story*** by Ben Carson- The director of Pediatric Neurosurgery at Johns Hopkins hospital details how he moved beyond a rough upbringing in inner city Detroit to become one of the world's great physicians.

5. ***Bonhoeffer: Pastor, Martyr, Prophet, Spy*** by Eric Metaxas- A look at the life of one of the great theologians of the 20th century who bravely stood up to Hitler in World War II Germany and produced some of the seminal literary works of the Christian faith.

6. ***Edison: A Biography*** by Matthew Josephson- Perhaps the greatest creator of modern times, Edison is credited with inventing the phonograph, the motion picture camera, and the light bulb. The shrewd businessman had 1,093 U.S. patents to his credit.

7. ***Health Care You Can Live With*** by Dr. Scott Morris- The founder of America's largest faith-based clinic for the uninsured tells the story of how The Church Health Center was created and offers advice for maintaining physical and spiritual balance.

8. ***The Autobiography of Martin Luther King, Jr.*** edited by Clayborne Carson- An amazing collection of King's letters, sermons, speeches and notes offers an insightful look at the Civil Rights leader's struggle to eradicate racism by peaceful means.

9. ***Truman*** by David McCullough- One of the most celebrated biographies of an American president offers remarkable insights on a wartime president who, while faced with some of the most difficult challenges of the 20th century, led with humility and courage.

10. ***Walt Disney: The Triumph of the American Imagination*** by Neal Gabler- The definitive work on one of the most consequential creators of our time. Disney reinvented the world of entertainment with his innovations in animation, theme parks, and merchandising.

TEDASHII

IDENTITY CRISIS

By Grant Guffin

> "I can't wait 'til I'm out of this
> house that I'm in,
> Cause every single day I feel
> trapped inside my skin,
> Every scratch, every crack,
> every spot on the exterior,
> Flaws that make me pause,
> I feel so inferior,
> I was seven when I felt it,
> I couldn't conceive it,
> Age eleven felt it again and
> that's when I believed it."
>
> (From *Burn This House Down* by Tedashii)

TEDASHII ANDERSON REMEMBERS LYING BENEATH THE STARS AND DREAMING. Not of becoming a college football player, though that would eventually happen. Not of someday meeting the girl of his dreams, marrying, and raising a family with her, though that would happen as well. Nor of making a successful career as a rapper, selling albums, and performing all over the world, though that would happen too.

No, Tedashii dreamed of meeting his father for the first time. And having a little brother. Of getting to know them, love them, and finally finding that missing piece of his identity. But that dream seemed as far away from southeast Texas, where Tedashii was raised by his mom and stepfather, as the stars themselves.

MUSIC WAS ALSO A CONSTANT IN THE HOME, AND BECAUSE OF HIS MOM'S AND STEPFATHER'S SHARED LOVE OF THE BLUES, ARTISTS LIKE BB KING, MILES DAVIS, AND OTIS REDDING PROVIDED THE SOUNDTRACK FOR TEDASHII'S CHILDHOOD ADVENTURES.

Education was the priority in the Anderson home, and Tedashii's mom, a schoolteacher, regularly drilled the importance of academics into her children. "Once you have it up here," she would say, pointing to her head, "no one can ever take it away from you." And so Tedashii formed a part of his identity by pushing himself in the classroom, working to be the kid with all the answers.

Music was also a constant in the home, and because of his mom's and stepfather's shared love of the blues, artists like BB King, Miles Davis, and Otis Redding provided the soundtrack for Tedashii's childhood adventures. Mrs. Anderson found the new brand of urban music popular among her son's peers—a style called hip hop—particularly distasteful. So the sound, with its explicit lyrics and promotion of gang violence and sexual exploits, was banned from the home.

But his mom's warnings only added to the music's mystique: "You couldn't get away from it," Tedashii explains. "It was always a part of where I grew up. It was good music to me." And so another piece of his identity was formed listening to and observing rappers like LL Cool J, NWA, and DJ Quik. "I loved how LL was intense and arrogant," he says. "I wore a Kangol, had my jeans rolled up, tongues sticking out of my shoes." And as he listened, he wondered, "Are these guys really living the lives they're describing? That's what the videos showed. No wonder my mom didn't want me to hear it."

But still, there was something about the hip hop vibe that resonated deeply with the young man. "The feeling you get from hearing a guy rhyme, watching a guy break to it, seeing how the crowd reacts...it was a dope feeling."

FINALLY WILLING TO SET ASIDE AN IDENTITY BUILT ON PERSONAL ACHIEVEMENT AND CULTURAL STATUS, TEDASHII BEGAN TO UNDERSTAND AND EXPERIENCE—FOR THE FIRST TIME IN HIS LIFE—THE UNCONDITIONAL LOVE OF A FATHER.

Tedashii is the product of an African-American mom and a Samoan dad. His parents met when they were both in the military, dated and conceived a child, but never married. They grew apart after his dad was stationed in Germany and his mom returned home to Texas. There were a few letters back and forth, and in one of them Tedashii's mom mentioned she might be pregnant. But Tedashii's dad decided to move on with his life before her suspicions were confirmed, and the two eventually lost touch.

Focusing his competitive, adolescent energies, Tedashii initially hoped to make a name for himself in academics and athletics. He earned a partial scholarship to Baylor for his schoolwork, and hoped to pay the rest of his tuition with scholarship money from football and track. But a back injury his freshman year led to the discovery of scoliosis—a curving of the spinal column—and in an instant those dreams were dashed.

"Advances made at me and I wouldn't receive it,
I tried to move on, but I'm stuck like cement,
And I felt so alone, man it's like this thing trapped me,
I played make believe to erase that it happened,
Every falling star, I'm wishin' for a change,
I need another place to live free from these chains"
(From *Burn This House Down* by Tedashii)

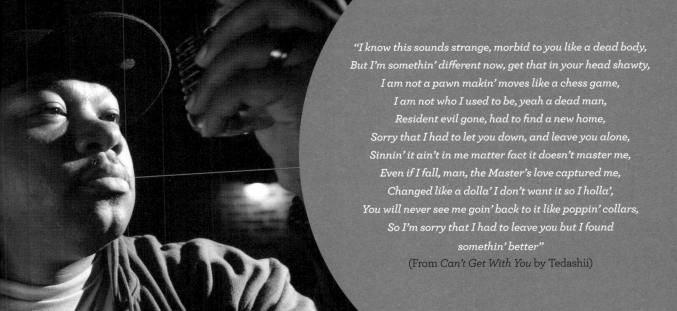

"I know this sounds strange, morbid to you like a dead body,
But I'm somethin' different now, get that in your head shawty,
I am not a pawn makin' moves like a chess game,
I am not who I used to be, yeah a dead man,
Resident evil gone, had to find a new home,
Sorry that I had to let you down, and leave you alone,
Sinnin' it ain't in me matter fact it doesn't master me,
Even if I fall, man, the Master's love captured me,
Changed like a dolla' I don't want it so I holla',
You will never see me goin' back to it like poppin' collars,
So I'm sorry that I had to leave you but I found
somethin' better"
(From *Can't Get With You* by Tedashii)

Lacking a plan for his life and now keenly aware of his own limitations, Tedashii was open when a friend shared the love and hope offered to all of us by God through Jesus. "When the injury happened, I saw my flaws," he explains. "I saw that with high points, there are also low points. Before then, I would've found the idea that I needed anyone other than myself offensive."

Finally willing to set aside an identity built on personal achievement and cultural status, Tedashii began to understand and experience—for the first time in his life—the unconditional love of a Father. He found guidance in God's Word. A source of help through prayer. Strength in the company of brothers. Correction and comfort in the Holy Spirit. A sense of purpose and fulfillment in being who he was created to be—a son of the King.

"I used to sit in the dorm and listen to Tupac and freestyle over it," Tedashii reminisces. "One day my friend who led me to Christ came in and heard me. He said, 'Why are you cursing so much?' I told him you have to curse when you rap. He challenged me to write a rap without any cursing. Then he told me to rewrite a rap with a particular subject, so I did. Then he said, 'Now come do the rap in this talent show I'm singing in.' I said, 'No way!'"

"Long story short, I did it," Tedashii laughs. "It was horrible. The worst rap ever. And it was about Jesus. Everybody was there—every fraternity and sorority, even the professors. But he knew what he was doing. He was challenging me to be distinct about my faith.

Tedashii relocated to Dallas, where he attended Denton Bible Church. A group of friends were being discipled there and working on music. Tedashii joined them and began taking rap seriously for the first time. "I started to write more and care about what I was saying," he says. "I wanted to make music that was creative enough that people would listen, but direct enough that people would know what I was saying."

Among his new friends was a rapper named Lecrae, who invited Tedashii to be a part of an album he was creating. "We wrote verses, but no one thought it would be a vocation," Tedashii explains. "We never thought it would go as far as it's gone. Pretty soon, we were doing tours with (music artists) Mercy Me and festivals with Casting Crowns."

Fast-forward through multiple albums, tours and concerts, today Tedashii finds himself with a platform to help other young men avoid the traps that sidetracked him in his formative years. "I'm tired of seeing 'boys with beards' in our urban culture," he says. "I want to see young men 'man-up' and look like Christ, not like boys. Cultivate. Don't live with envy. Live the life we've been called out to live. Learn from past seasons and prepare for the future."

Growing in his newfound faith, making music, and at home among friends who shared his passion for both, Tedashii was finally at peace. But another surprise was in store. "Keenan, the friend who led me to Christ, said one day, 'Why don't you try to find your real father?' I told him, 'My mom always said you never miss something you never had.' He said, 'You found your heavenly Father and you were missing out on a lot. I imagine who you are now would only be enhanced by finding your earthly father. Plus, if he's not a Christian, you get to share the Gospel with your dad.' So I was like, 'Oh. Yeah, let me do that.'"

"I called the Geraldo show when they had a special on reuniting families," Tedashii explains. "They hooked me up with a company in Beverly Hills. The woman who answered the phone...was so moved by my story that she paid for the service herself. Two weeks later, I got a letter with a list of the people they could find in the States. So I wrote letters to all those addresses... and one of them happened to be an uncle. He connected me with an aunt...who knew of me based on the fact that my dad had somewhat known of me. She gave me an address and I wrote him a letter."

"I got six letters back—from my dad and my five siblings— four sisters...and a younger brother. My dad told me he was a pastor. He was in a proud state; I was in a surreal, joyous state. It was dope."

> *"It. Is. Wonderful,*
> *And man no feeling can describe it,*
> *And even though I try to there's little*
> *that can define it,*
> *Any emotions like a potion be*
> *controlling me,*
> *Island Ocean living when these visions*
> *get a hold of me,*
> *Yea, interest to the King of kings,*
> *And I don't need a rosary,*
> *All I need is Him, Him, Him,*
> *Who I need?*
> *The One that exist in Three,*
> *And not for me but for His glory,*
> *It's Him and not me He the star of*
> *this story"*
> (From *That Will Be the Day* by Tedashii)

In time, Tedashii traveled to his dad's home in Hawaii and met his new family face-to-face. As they got to know one another, he felt a special closeness to his younger brother Jay. "I met him when he was 14," Tedashii says. "He asked about staying with me (in the mainland) and my dad also suggested it. He ended up staying all the way through high school."

Being a guardian to Jay presented its share of challenges, but living under the same roof allowed the two brothers to make up for lost time. Tedashii says the experience was a valuable lesson in responsibility, "When you have a little charisma, favor with people, they'll give you a pass on responsibility, until your lack of responsibility affects them directly. My brother showing up was the reason I couldn't hide any longer; when it affected him it affected me. It caused me to have forethought, to think beyond where we were to where we wanted to go." Tedashii took the initiative to create and cultivate.

These days, Tedashii maintains a close relationship with his extended family, while leading and caring for a family of his own. He believes his life experiences have equipped him to teach others, particularly urban young men, to be effective creators and cultivators. "My wanting to speak into their situation is because my heart is for them," he offers.

"I'd shock them by telling them you're not special because you have it bad. I thought the world was owed to me because I had it bad when I was a kid. I had to accept the fact that there's a God who's all-powerful, all-knowing, all-loving. I had to meet him before I could find out who I was meant to be as a creator and a cultivator. There's contentment in Christ you won't find in a girl, or the clubs you go to. I don't need all that 'cause I really am satisfied." ⊞

Watch Tedashii create and cultivate at the end of session 6

Manhood Definition

SESSION **THREE** | Training Guide **NOTES**

Manhood Definition

I. **INTRODUCTION**

1. In the last session we learned that God designed men to follow His example and to _____, specifically by creating and cultivating.

2. Most importantly we learned in the last session that the type of manhood God created us to live cannot be done with our **self-effort**. Only a real, vibrant relationship with Jesus Christ can provide us with the fuel we need to live out Authentic Manhood.

    Online video at authenticmanhood.com

II. **THREE AREAS OF RESPONSIBILITY**

1. God gave man a_____ to obey.

    *   God have us a will greater than our own to obey.

2. God gave man a **work** to do.

    *   Follow God's example to create and cultivate.

3. God gave man a _____to love.

    *   A companion for intimacy and fellowship.

III. FIRST ADAM / SECOND ADAM

1. The Bible describes _____ as the second Adam.[1]

    - Romans 5:17–19 "For if, because of one man's trespass [Adam], death reigned through that one man, much more will those who receive the abundance of grace and the free gift of righteousness reign in life through the one man Jesus Christ ... For as by the one man's disobedience [Adam] the many were made sinners, so by the one man's obedience the many will be made righteous." (ESV)

        ○ Through Adam, sin entered the world, but through Jesus, _____ entered the world.

        ○ Jesus _____ the responsibilities of the first Adam, who failed miserably.

    - 1 Corinthians 15:45–47 "Thus it is written, the first man, Adam became a living being; the last Adam became a life-giving spirit... the first man was from the earth, a man of dust; the second man is from heaven." (ESV)

2. Every man will walk in the shadow of one of these two men.

3. The first Adam chose "_____ manhood." It's a manhood based on personal instinct, human reason, or human reaction.

4. Jesus is the example of _____ manhood.

[1] Jesus is called the "last Adam" and the "second man" in 1 Cor 15:45–47.

SESSION THREE | MANHOOD DEFINITION

IV. A COMPELLING DEFINITION OF AUTHENTIC MANHOOD

1. Reject _____

- Adam was passive in the garden:

    ○ "So when the woman saw that the tree was good for food, and that it was a delight to the eyes... she took of its fruit and ate, and she also gave some to her husband who was with her, and he ate." Genesis 3:6 (ESV)

- Jesus rejected passivity:

    ○ "Jesus, who, though he was in the form of God, did not count equality with God a thing to be grasped, but made himself nothing, taking the form of a servant, being born in the likeness of men. And being found in human form, he humbled himself by becoming obedient to the point of death, even death on a cross." Philippians 2:5–9 (ESV)

2. Accept _____

- Adam failed in the three specific responsibilities that were given to him by God.

    ○ Jesus accepted responsibility for a *will to obey:*

        ◆ "My food is to do the will of him who sent me and to accomplish his work." John 4:34 (ESV)

    ○ Jesus accepted responsibility for a *work to do:*

        ◆ "I [Jesus] glorified you [God] on earth, having accomplished the work that you game me to do." John 17:4 (ESV)

    ○ Jesus accepted responsibility for a *woman to love:*

        ◆ "Husbands, love your wives, as Christ loved the church and gave himself up for her." Ephesians 5:25 (ESV)

3. Lead _____

- Adam failed to lead in the garden.

- Jesus led by providing direction for others. He told His disciples "follow me." Matthew 4:19 (ESV)

- Jesus led by providing protection for others. He said "I am the good shepherd. The good shepherd lays down his life for the sheep." John 10:11 (ESV)

- Jesus led by providing life for others: "the first man Adam became a living being; the last Adam [Jesus] became a life-giving spirit." 1 Corinthians 15:45 (ESV)

4. _____ Eternally

- Adam invested in the temporary, choosing what would satisfy him in the moment.

- Jesus invested in the eternal. He lived it and He taught it.

  - In Matthew 6:19–20, He said "Do not lay up for yourselves treasures on earth, where moth and rust destroy and where thieves break in and steal, but lay up for yourselves treasures in heaven, where neither moth nor rust destroys and where thieves do not break in and steal." (ESV)

v. CONCLUSION

1. Authentic men:

- Reject passivity

- Accept responsibility

- Lead courageously

- Invest eternally

2. It's hopeless to live this out without the _____ spirit of Jesus fueling your journey.

DISCUSSION / REFLECTION QUESTIONS

1. React to the definition of manhood given today. Is it one you can adopt for your life? Why or why not?

2. How does the original manhood design (create and cultivate) from the last session relate to the manhood definition of this session?

3. When have you seen passivity in your own life? Are there any areas where you are currently struggling with passivity?

4. How are you investing eternally?

A Clear Vision for Authentic Manhood By Tierce Green

When I moved to Texas, one of the first things I discovered while driving east on Interstate 30 was the ability to see miles ahead of me to where I was going. A clear view of the Dallas skyline confirmed that I was headed in the right direction.

I experienced the opposite extreme somewhere outside of Lubbock when a sand and dust storm reduced visibility to a level where street signs, traffic lights, trucks and cars just blended together. I had no choice but to pull over and wait for it to pass. It sounded as if the paint was being sandblasted from my car.

In my quest for Authentic Manhood, I have experienced a mix of feeling my way and finding my way. As a man, I have felt sandblasted and defeated on the side of the road; and I have found direction and clarity that is bigger than Dallas.

Accurate directions and clear vision are essential in the journey towards Authentic Manhood. In *The 7 Habits of Highly Effective People,* by Stephen Covey, Habit #2 is to "begin with the end in mind."[1] The truth in that principle resonates with practical applications for manhood. It calls for clarity, direction and intentionality at the outset. A clearly defined path will take us where we want to go in our quest for Authentic Manhood.

You've heard the saying, "If you aim at nothing, you'll hit it every time."[2] That was my reality all through my teenage years and early twenties. I never had a real connection with my dad. He died when I was ten, and I grew up with a single mom. While grateful for her strength and encouragement, I was clueless when it came to understanding what it meant to be a man. With girls, cars, money, friends, sports and matters of character, I just gave it my best shot. Manhood for me was hit or miss with a lot of misses. I either aimed at nothing or the targets I aimed at were always changing.

I put my faith in Jesus Christ at the end of the summer following my freshman year of college. I wish I could say that a switch was flipped, and I instantly became a real man. But, it's not that simple. Authentic Manhood is a process. There is no such thing as microwave manhood.

My perception of what it meant to be a Christian man had been skewed by the way Jesus was typically presented in my church experience. David Murrow says in his book *Why Men Hate Going To*

> *"...our very definition of what it means to be a 'good Christian' skews female."*

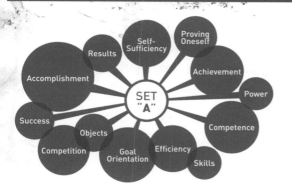

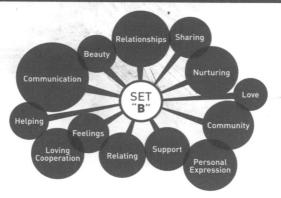

¹ Stephen R. Covey, *The 7 Habits of Highly Effective People* (Simon & Schuster, 1989), p. 95. | ³ David Murrow, *Why Men Hate Going to Church, Revised Edition* (Thomas Nelson, 2011), chapter 1. | ⁴ John Gray, PhD, *Men Are from Mars, Women Are from Venus* (HarperCollins, 1992), chapter 1. | ⁵ Mark 8:22-24 (NIV). | ⁶,⁷ Ibid | ⁴ Author unknown. | ⁷ 33-The Series, *The Definition of Manhood* (Authentic Manhood, Fellowship Associates, 2011).

Church, "our very definition of what it means to be a 'good Christian' skews female."³ He illustrates and supports this position with a quiz. Here it is:

Murrow says that he has administered this quiz to thousands of people: men, women, Christians and non-Christians. More than 90 percent of the time, people choose Set "B" as the best representation of Jesus Christ and His values.

Then, he reveals the origin of the two lists. These two value sets were plucked from the pages of the best-selling book, *Men Are from Mars, Women Are from Venus by* Dr. John Gray. In Chapter 1, he identifies Set "A" as the values of Mars, whereas Set "B" describes the values of Venus.⁴ In other words, Set "A" represents the values common among men while Set "B" represents the values common among women.

Most of the people who took this little quiz think of Christ as having the values that come naturally to a woman! Granted, the values listed in Set "B" are some of the values that represented Jesus. The results of this quiz illustrate how confused today's culture is about the real Jesus and the kind of masculinity he modeled. Most people's vision of biblical manhood is blurred.

When Jesus and His disciples were traveling through the town of Bethsaida, some people brought a blind man to Him. Jesus took him by the hand and led him outside the village. He then spit on the man's eyes, touched him and asked, "Do you see anything?"⁵

The man looked up and said, "I see people; they look like trees walking around."⁶ He could see; but, he couldn't see clearly. People were blurred and undefined. That's a pretty good description of what a lot of men see when they consider what it means to be a man. Their vision is blurred and undefined.

The Scriptures say in Mark 8:25 (NIV), "Once more Jesus put his hands on the man's eyes. Then his eyes were opened, his sight was restored, and he saw everything clearly."

To maintain a clear vision of Authentic Manhood, it takes more than a brief encounter to discover what Jesus is really like. ***He is our model for manhood, and that demands our full attention.*** A close look at the life of Jesus reveals that real men reject passivity, accept responsibility, lead courageously and invest eternally.⁷ Those are powerful and compelling statements! They look good written in a journal, but integrating them into your life requires discipline, vulnerability, trust and accountability over time.

Every man needs accurate directions and clear vision. What do you see? 33

33 THE SERIES™

FOOD FOR THOUGHT

QUOTES TO CONSIDER WHEN PROCESSING THE MANHOOD DEFINITION AND HOW YOU SHOULD RESPOND TO IT.

REJECT PASSIVITY

"The impossible is often the untried." —JIM GOODWIN

"To him who is determined it remains only to act." —ITALIAN PROVERB

"The difference between a successful person and others is not a lack of strength, not a lack of knowledge, but a lack of will." —VINCE LOMBARDI

"The most difficult thing is the decision to act. The rest is merely tenacity... The process is its own reward." —ROBYN DAVIDSON

ACCEPT RESPONSIBILITY

"It is not only what we do, but also what we do not do for which we are accountable." —MOLI

"You cannot escape the responsibility of tomorrow by evading it today." —ABRAHAM LINCOLN

"The willingness to accept responsibility for one's own life is the source from which self-respect springs." —JOAN DIDION

"To be a man is to be responsible. It is to feel shame at the sight of what seems to be unmerited misery. It is take pride in a victory won by one's comrades. It is to feel, when settin one's stone, that one is contributi to the building of the world." —ANTOINE DE SAINT-EXUPERY

LEAD COURAGEOUSLY

"Courage is being scared to death... and saddling up anyway."
—JOHN WAYNE

"Courage is contagious. When a brave man takes a stand, the spines of others are often stiffened."
—BILLY GRAHAM

"Man cannot discover new oceans unless he has the courage to lose sight of the shore." —LORD CHESTERFIELD

"The courage we desire and prize is not the courage to die decently, but to live manfully." —THOMAS CARLYLE

INVEST ETERNALLY

"Where I was born and where and how I have lived is unimportant. It is what I have done with where I have been that should be of interest."
—DWIGHT L. MOODY

"We are not cisterns made for hoarding, we are channels made for sharing." —BILLY GRAHAM

"He is no fool who gives what he cannot keep to gain what he cannot lose." —JIM ELLIOT

YOUNG ENTREPRENEUR INVESTS ETERNALLY

by Grant Guffin

EMBRACING THE MANHOOD DEFINITION

Todd Brogdon was conventional manhood's definition of a success. A venture capitalist, he was well on his way to financial independence. He and his wife, Jessica, were raising two healthy children in a nice home in a comfortable suburb, with both sets of parents nearby to help. They were active members of their church and community. A sports fan, he was a short road trip away from his favorite sports team; so game weekends with the guys were no tall order.

AND THEN THE PHONE RANG.

A BUSINESS ASSOCIATE, DABBS CAVIN, WAS ON THE OTHER END OF THE LINE.

Though they barely knew one another, Dabbs had a proposal for Todd to consider: "He mentioned this idea of microfinance," Todd explains, "and that he was considering moving to Rwanda to start a bank. He asked me to consider coming along to help get it started." Dabbs didn't really know Todd, but said that in his search for the best fit, Todd's name continued to surface.

Todd agreed to consider the idea, figuring it would be nothing more than an interesting dinner conversation topic for him and his wife. Todd had never been to Rwanda—or anywhere else outside the United States for that matter—short of brief vacation excursions across the border into Canada and Mexico. He couldn't place Rwanda on a map if he tried, so the idea of leaving everything he had ever known to start a bank in a poor African nation seemed nothing short of ridiculous.

REJECT PASSIVITY.

Todd remembered this component of the manhood definition from his Men's Fraternity experience years earlier. It was a concept that, unfortunately, fit this situation. If he were truly going to pursue Authentic Manhood, he would at least consider the new opportunity, as outlandish as it seemed. He recalled a conversation with a friend just days earlier when he had pondered aloud how one knows when God is speaking. Todd guessed he was the type who would require a hammer over the head to know for sure.

"Maybe Dabbs's phone call was the hammer," he thought. Then cold chills ran down his spine. "Oh please, God, no. I have NO desire to go to Rwanda."

He picked up the phone and called Jessica, told her perhaps they should give the idea consideration. "What am I saying?" Jessica started to cry. She was thinking the same thing. They decided to seek counsel from people they trusted, hoping to hear, "That sounds wonderful, but you've got two small kids. You're in the best part of your career. It's probably not a good idea to relocate to Africa." Instead, they received the same response from each: "This sounds like a great opportunity. A great adventure."

"OH BOY..."

Todd was growing increasingly desperate. He began researching malaria, hoping that information would scare him back to his senses. Then, in August 2005, Dabbs and his family committed to the effort. The Cavins relocated to Rwanda in April 2006. Four days later, Todd and his family followed—but only for a visit. "We spent a week there," Todd recalls, "and even though it was way out of our comfort zone, we decided that week to make the commitment."

In August 2006, Todd and his family relocated to Rwanda for what would ultimately become a two-year effort to build a microfinance bank. The organization through which the bank was being launched provided cultural training to make the transition easier, but it was still a challenge to adjust to cultural and language barriers and the absence of luxuries that made life simpler back home. But Todd and his family pushed forward, acclimating to their host country as he and Dabbs attacked their mission. **Todd had refused to sit by passively while the people of Rwanda lived in poverty.**

Microfinance is the concept of making small business loans—typically $50-$200—to people who have no actual collateral

ACCEPT RESPONSIBILITY.

or assets. Loans are made to individuals, but repayment of the loan is an obligation shared collectively by what are sometimes referred to as "trust groups." If someone is unable or unwilling to repay their loan, members of the group must pool their resources to repay it on their behalf. Peer pressure, integrity and a sense of personal pride are typically the motivators for following through on one's repayment.

Most of those on the receiving end of micro loans are women. All manner of businesses are launched by these fledgling entrepreneurs, and the results have allowed numerous citizens of third world countries a dignified means of providing for their families and contributing to their communities that they would not have had otherwise.

"The idea is it's one spoke in the big wheel of the access to capital for all," Todd says. "The vast majority of our culture here (in the United States) has access to a bank where they can save money...a place where they can borrow money to buy a vehicle or whatever they need. In a place like Rwanda, the only people who had access to that were the one or two percent who were wealthy."

Todd, Dabbs and their team accepted a responsibility that was especially complex and often overwhelming, but as the bank took root in the community, people made the most of the opportunities they were given. "You saw (successes) in every group," Todd reflects. "In every group there were always women and men who were able to leverage this...and really do something special...and really change their lives in a significant way."

Because Todd accepted responsibility for laying the groundwork properly, he was able to hand a healthy bank over to those who could take it to even greater effectiveness.

LEAD COURAGEOUSLY.

His work with the bank complete, Todd and his family returned to the United States in 2008. Once home, a mutual friend connected him to an entrepreneur starting a coffee exporting business...in Rwanda. Five minutes after meeting the entrepreneur, Todd was offered a role with the new business.

The company later purchased a coffee roasting plant in the United States, and the Westrock Coffee brand was born. Now CEO of the company, Todd has helped foster relationships with some of the world's largest retailers. If all goes as planned, Westrock Coffee will someday populate store shelves around the world, creating new markets—and much-needed economic development—for Rwandan coffee growers, those with whom they do business and on and on.

Todd hopes his business will provide sound, courageous leadership for other businesses in a country where positive examples have been in short supply. **"We're a for-profit venture trying to do the right thing and make a difference on the ground,"** Todd explains. **"We want to show people if you do business the right way, treat people right, and follow the rules, you can be successful.** Over here (in the United States), we're trying to tell the story of what's going on over there—and let people know that a practical way that they can be a part of it is to buy Westrock Coffee."

Todd returns to Rwanda two or three times a year to see his operation in person, form new relationships with potential partners, and visit old friends. Because he leads his company courageously and with integrity, the Rwandan business community may be impacted for generations by the example of an honest broker and the economic development he provides.

INVEST ETERNALLY

Todd Brogdon may no longer be conventional manhood's definition of success. He's fine with that. He's much happier living the life of Authentic Manhood. Rejecting passivity. Accepting responsibility. Leading courageously.

And yes...investing eternally.

For Todd, following his specific path to Authentic Manhood meant relocating to a strange and distant place. But he's quick to point out that the roadmap for a man isn't a one-size-fits-all deal. "Maybe everyone isn't supposed to care about a Rwandan guy living in a village somewhere," Todd says. "But I've always been an underdog guy. I'm rooting for the guy who's not supposed to be on top. That's what I feel for the Rwandans. They're the underdog, the fighter. And if there's any way I could play a role in seeing their lives changed—to me, that's where God put me."

"You could have the same story about a guy who's working in the inner city and making a significant difference there," he adds. "For me, when I was comfortable and things felt secure...I used to say, 'Man, I don't see God at work very much.' **I had this sense I must be doing something right because life was easy. But that's skewed thinking."**

"What I've seen through all of this upheaval is that God seems to move when you're not comfortable, when you don't have everything figured out, when there is a level of risk. And that kind of goes back to the definition of what faith is."

From a quiet life of complacency in the suburbs to a life of adventure spanning two continents. Todd Brogdon has embraced the definition of Authentic Manhood. 33

The **Four Faces** of **Manhood**
PART ONE: **KING / WARRIOR**

SESSION **FOUR** | Training Guide **NOTES**

The **Four Faces** of **Manhood**
PART ONE: **KING / WARRIOR**

I. **INTRODUCTION**

1. In the next two sessions we're going to give you a perspective of masculinity that **compliments** and expands our manhood definition.

2. Unfortunately, society has often depicted masculinity as _____.

3. We need a biblically-based, broad masculinity that is _____
   —the kind of masculinity that can move into multiple settings and express itself appropriately and powerfully when needed.

4. Over the next two sessions, we are going to introduce you to the Four Faces of Manhood.[1] In this session, we'll examine the **King** Face and the **Warrior** Face.

II. **THE KING FACE** | LEADING WITH INTEGRITY

1. The King Face reflects _____ energy.

   - Characterized by:

     ○ Strong conviction

     ○ Courageous moral choices

     ○ Servant's spirit

     ○ Righteous leadership

---

[1] *This session has been influenced by Stu Weber, "Four Pillars of a Man's Heart: Bringing Strength into Balance" (Multnomah, 1997). The Four Faces of Manhood are not necessarily intended to reflect only psychological categories, but rather are a point of reference to discuss the various roles, responsibilities, and relationships experienced by most men.*

- Its essence is:
  - Providing for others
  - Loving what is right

2. The King Face is primarily associated with **integrity**.

3. Good examples of the King Face, both from the Old Testament:

- Nathan

- King _____

4. The King Face is also associated with _____.

5. Caricatures of the King Face

- If a man's King Face is pushed too far, he can become a bully, tyrant, or dictator –
  The **Tyrant**.

- If a man does not have enough of the King Face, he can struggle with compromise –
  The _____.

6. The King Face – leading with integrity.

III. **THE WARRIOR FACE** | FIGHTING FOR WHAT MATTERS MOST

1. The Warrior Face reflects _____ energy.

- Characterized by:

    ○   Initiative

    ○   Protection

    ○   Provision

    ○   Perseverance

2. The Warrior Face is primarily associated with **initiative**.

3. The Warrior Face fights for what _____ most.

4. It is also associated with **purpose**.

5. 1 Corinthians 9:24-27 – Run the race to win. Fight for the _____ things and eternal things.

6. 1 Tim. 11:12 – Fight the good fight of the **Faith**.

7. Caricatures of the Warrior Face:

   • If a man's Warrior Face is pushed too far, he can become abusive and harsh to those around him – The **Destroyer**.

   • If a man does not have enough of the Warrior Face, he can struggle with passivity. He easily gives up and is quick to tap out or surrender – The _____.

8. The Warrior Face – Fighting for what matters most.

IV. CONCLUSION

1. The _____ Face and the _____ Face are the first two faces of manhood. Authentic Manhood must have both. It has to have righteous energy and courageous energy. We must "lead with integrity" and be willing to "fight for what matters most."

2. The next session will examine the next two faces of manhood: the Face of the **Lover** and the Face of the **Friend**.

DISCUSSION / REFLECTION QUESTIONS

1. What are some typical, one-dimensional caricatures of masculinity? How can this affect our view of manhood?

2. Do you identify more with the King Face or the Warrior Face? Why?

3. Has your integrity ever been tested? Under stress, are you more likely to be a tyrant or a compromiser?

4. Is it easy for you to take the initiative? Are you taking initiative in the right areas? Under stress, are you more likely to be a destroyer or a wimp?

SUPPORTING RESOURCES

Weber, Stu. *Four Pillars of a Man's Heart: Bringing Strength into Balance.* Multnomah, 1997.

The content in the supporting resource above does not necessarily reflect the opinion of Authentic Manhood. Readers should use recommended resources but form their own opinions.

The Price of Progress By John Bryson

Significant things have a significant cost. Manhood is not achieved without some sort of price to pay. Every time a man grows his King or Warrior Face, he is growing courageously and using a righteous energy.

Think about the King Face and how it relates to relationships between men. A man can either boldly set high standards or be passive and take shortcuts. Authentic men must operate with integrity and do what is right, rather than what is easy. *In doing so, men are immediately placing themselves in the minority and step out of mainstream manhood.* Isolation can quickly seep in, along with ridicule. Men around us will probably feel intimidated and may

act out in anger or jealousy. Though the King in you is never looking to embarrass or belittle other men, a byproduct of our noble steps will often expose the uglier side of others. Our high standards and lifestyle pursuits will often contrast with other men who do not mind cutting corners or compromising ethics to get ahead.

I remember my first job in a restaurant when I was a young man. A mentor at the time really challenged me to make sure that my work ethic was strong and growing. So, I became committed to doing that. I did that job with all the hard work I could muster. It took about two days of hard work before the other men working in the kitchen took me outside to "set me straight." *They basically told me to slow down and stop working so hard. Thankfully, I decided to lead with courage.* As politely as I could, I let them know I was not going to slack off. I decided to work hard, regardless of how that made them look or feel.

The same can be true when we put on our Warrior Face. When we take intentional steps away from mediocrity and create a new normal that is bold and full of initiative, we expose other men stuck in

TEN CLASSIC KING/WARRIOR MOVIES

Ten great films guaranteed to have you and your buddies ready to conquer the world...or at least give one another a spirited chest bump. Send the wife and kids to the mall, invite the guys over, fire up the grill, and adjourn to the man cave for these flicks:

1. **BRAVEHEART** (1995)- Starring Mel Gibson as 13th century warrior William Wallace, who is stirred to action by the murder of his wife. Wallace eventually leads his men into an epic battle for Scottish independence. | **Best line:** "...they may take our lives, but they will never take our freedom!"

2. **UNFORGIVEN** (1992)- Clint Eastwood is William Munny, an aging outlaw of the Old West, called back into action to deal with a corrupt sheriff and two cowboys inflicting harm on local women. | **Best line:** "Any man don't wanna get killed better clear on out the back."

3. **THE DIRTY DOZEN** (1967)- Lee Marvin, Charles Bronson and Jim Brown are part of a team of convicted felons given an opportunity at retribution via a suicide mission on the eve of the D-Day invasion of World War II. | **Best line:** "You've got one religious maniac, one malignant dwarf, two near-idiots, and the rest I don't even wanna think about!"

4. **BEN-HUR** (1959)- Charlton Heston is the title character, a wealthy merchant betrayed and taken captive by a childhood friend. Ben-Hur seeks to repay his captor, and is deeply moved by a compassionate stranger in the process. | **Best line:** "You may conquer the land, you may slaughter the people. That is not the end. We will rise again."

mediocrity. *Swimming upstream can be lonely and can make you feel crazy, especially in the beginning.* My advice is to stay the course! Any new, bold and courageous step will inevitably have a time of uncertainty and unsettledness. As a Warrior we must not be surprised when we take on a few arrows. That's the price that may come with putting on a Warrior Face.

Ultimately, the benefits of being a Warrior far outweigh whatever price tag you have to pay. I guarantee you that the Warrior steps you take will inspire and create a tribe of men around you who will all want to live just like you do.

For me, hearing about men who "man up" and put on their Warrior Face always speaks to something deep within my core and inspires me. When I hear of other men stepping out and creating "new normals" such as losing 40 pounds, getting out of debt, finding a better job, writing a book, or navigating and leading their child through a tough season, it showcases men in the best of light.

In reality, we are fallen men in a fallen world and we must learn to wear the Warrior Face in every area of our life. Chaos and brokenness are all around us. Every day, week, month, year and season of our life is an opportunity to step up with courage and create something noble and good. We then leave passivity, chaos, could-have-beens and nothingness in the dust behind us.

A part of putting on the Warrior Face and using the courageous energy God gives each of us is about playing offense rather than defense. *Be bold!* 33

> *I guarantee you that the Warrior steps you take will inspire and create a tribe of men around you who will all want to live just like you do.*

5. **ROCKY** (1976) Sylvester Stallone is down-and-out Philadelphia boxer Rocky Balboa, given a shot at the heavyweight title in what is supposed to be a one-sided match-up in favor of champ Apollo Creed. | **Best line:** "You're gonna eat lightning and you're gonna crap thunder!"

6. **BULLITT** (1968)- Steve McQueen is Bullitt, a San Francisco police lieutenant assigned to protect a mob informant prior to trial. Hit men, car chases and elaborate deception pit one man against forces of evil. | **Best line:** "Sell whatever you want, but don't sell it here tonight."

7. **GLADIATOR** (2000)- Russell Crowe is General Maximus, a second century warrior taken captive by the evil Emperor Commodus. Maximus is put to the ultimate test by an antagonist jealous of his popularity and determined to destroy him. | **Best line:** "My name is Maximus...and I will have my vengeance in this life or the next."

8. **THE MAGNIFICENT SEVEN** (1960) or its Japanese predecessor, The Seven Samurai (1954)- Yul Brenner and Steve McQueen are among seven American gunmen hired to protect a small village in Mexico from a group of malicious bandits. | **Best line:** "Nobody throws me my guns and says run. Nobody."

9. **THE LORD OF THE RINGS: THE FELLOWSHIP OF THE RING** (2001)- Elijah Wood and Viggo Mortensen are Frodo and Aragorn, inhabitants of Middle-earth, a place where a Ring is the representation of evil. The two friends and their companions must overcome evil Orcs and the Dark Lord to destroy the ring at Mt. Doom. | **Best line:** "If by my life or death I can protect you I will. You have my sword..."

10. **THE UNTOUCHABLES** (1987) Kevin Costner as Elliott Ness, Sean Connery as Jimmy Malone, and Robert DeNiro as Al Capone. Ness and his team battle rampant corruption and attempt to take down violent mobster Capone. | **Best line:** "I wanna start taking the fight to him! I wanna hurt Capone!"

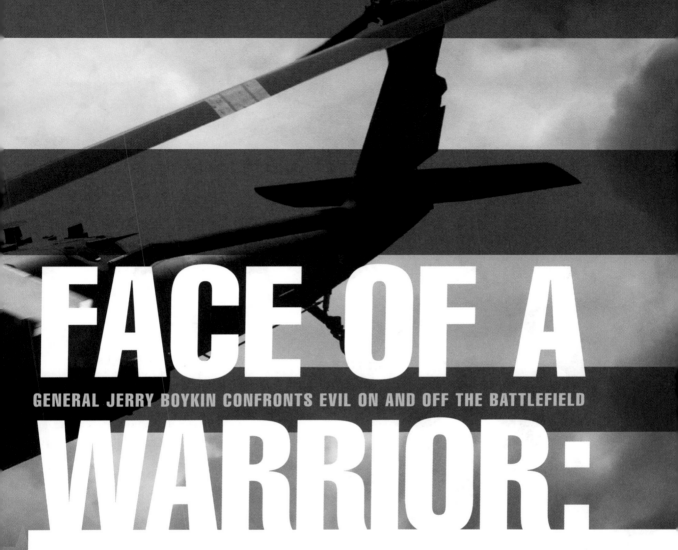

FACE OF A WARRIOR:

GENERAL JERRY BOYKIN CONFRONTS EVIL ON AND OFF THE BATTLEFIELD

COLONEL JERRY BOYKIN WAS DISTRAUGHT. Hours earlier he'd commanded Delta Force in a joint special operation in the Battle of Mogadishu—later depicted in the Hollywood film *Black Hawk Down*. Their mission, to capture leaders of the Habr Gidr clan led by Somali warlord Mohamed Farrah Aidid, had taken a horrible turn when two U.S. helicopters were felled by rocket-propelled grenades.

Instead of congratulating his soldiers on the completion of another successful mission, Jerry had watched as blood flowed like a stream from the back of a military truck filled with bodies of the dead and wounded. The conflict was, at that time, the bloodiest since the Vietnam War, with 15 of Jerry's warriors killed, 70 wounded, and five whose corpses were dragged through the streets of Mogadishu as macabre trophies.

That night, alone in his bunk with his thoughts, Jerry confronted the question he'd been suppressing most of the day: **"GOD, WHERE ARE YOU?"**

Jerry answered his own question—lashing out with anger: "You were nowhere! Because you're not there! For twenty-three years I've been living a lie!"

Then, in the quiet, almost immediately, a comforting inner voice reminded him, "If there's no God, there's no hope." A simple but firm reminder that, in the midst of the enormous evil and brokenness surrounding him, God was there. Still at work. Still powerful. Still completely in control.

Much was lost in Somalia over that two-day period in October 1993. The horrific events of The Battle of Mogadishu left a permanent imprint on Jerry's soul. But in one of life's darkest hours he'd come to understand a profound truth: Life wouldn't always turn out as he hoped. His job was simply to be faithful.

Jerry knew from an early age he was destined for United States military service. It was the family business, after all—his father and four of his uncles having served in the military during World War II. It was one of the most honorable ways to spend a life, in Jerry's view, protecting the country against its enemies and defending the Constitution.

And so, upon earning a degree from Virginia Tech, Jerry was commissioned as a second lieutenant in the U.S. Army, with a determination and maturity uncommon among most young men. "I was probably more serious about (military service) than some," he explains.

"Integrity was a major issue to me, and I believed that the people under my charge deserved the very best. I also knew **I had an obligation because of my Christian faith and role as a Warrior in God's army to serve in a way that would reflect positively on my Savior."**

Jerry ascended quickly through the ranks, holding positions in the 2nd Armored Division, 101st Airborne, and as a Company Commander in the 24th Infantry (Mechanized). But the creation of an elite unit within the Army called Delta Force would take his life in a new, exciting and extremely dangerous direction.

Delta Force was formed in response to a number of terrorist incidents in the 1970s. Its founder, Colonel Charles Beckwith, was charged with the creation of a team for counter-terrorism, direct action, and national intervention operations capable of performing covert missions, including rescuing hostages and raids. Arguably the nation's most elite military unit, Delta Force was charged with operations that required a lion's courage and a surgeon's skill.

Jerry was given the opportunity to earn his spot with Beckwith's unit and ultimately became one of the founding members of a force that would become the stuff of legend. He excelled in his new calling, and in the years that followed found himself fighting in many of the world's hot spots.

One of his first high profile missions was in April 1980, as operations officer of Operation Eagle Claw, an attempt to free 53 Americans held hostage by followers of Iran's Ayatollah Khomeini. The mission was ultimately a failure, resulting in the deaths of eight U.S. servicemen, but Jerry believes he saw God perform a miracle that day.

"About 100 miles from Tehran we landed in the desert to refuel our helicopters before the last leg of the operation," Jerry recalls. "We were refueling from these C-130 aircraft, and right before we launched out we got all our men together and prayed. I led the prayer and asked God to go with us. We loaded up and began lifting off. As one of the helicopters lifted off, the pilot got vertigo, lost his equilibrium and crashed into the C-130."

"Forty-five of those men who stood there and prayed with me were trapped hopelessly inside the C-130 and couldn't get out. The whole thing was engulfed in flames and there was no question they were going to die. As I stood there about 100 feet away pleading with God not to let them all die, a door opened and all of a sudden they came running through the flames across the desert." In Jerry's view, it was a miracle—plain and simple.

Through his involvement with Delta Force, Jerry was involved in other historic missions including Operation Urgent Fury in Grenada in 1983, during which he took a .50 caliber round in the arm; the capture of Panamanian dictator Manuel Noriega in 1989; an early 1990s mission to capture Colombian drug lord Pablo Escobar.

"THERE WAS NO QUESTION THEY WERE GOING TO DIE."

He has seen, and confronted, much evil in the world. But he offers a word of caution to those who might think it's only the job of those in uniform to fight for what's right. Jerry believes every man is called to be a Warrior, to fight the good fight.

"There are many things in our society that are simply evil, but men are unwilling to take a stand and confront evil because they don't want to be criticized, because they've been led to believe the only answer to evil is to turn the other cheek," Jerry says. "Too often the church itself hasn't recognized that men are born with a Warrior spirit—it isn't recognized or rewarded. People have an innate sense of right and wrong, of justice, a willingness to take risks, to protect

LTG (Ret) Jerry Boykin

the innocent and fight for a just cause. When you go back and look at the message of turning the other cheek, it wasn't a message of passivity. It was a message of service."

"We talk about the love of Christ, but don't talk about the fact that Christ told his disciples **'if you don't have a sword, sell your cloak and buy one.'** (Luke 22:36) Jesus wasn't saying, 'Build my Kingdom with a sword', He was saying that, in building His Kingdom, you may have to defend yourself and protect others. Men are instinctively Warriors, and we need to nurture and use it in the right way."

Just as General Jerry Boykin is actively calling today's men to put on the Warrior Face to confront evil, he also believes men can avoid creating evil to begin with by wearing the King Face. With that in mind, he's launched an organization called Kingdom Warriors, to challenge men to live according to God's standard—rooting

Scripture, when we're in a situation that requires a rapid response we have every reason to expect God is going to lead us, to give us the right skills and abilities, the right answers to perplexing and complex problems."

"Where we get in trouble is when we become arrogant, lose our humility and begin to rely on ourselves," Jerry says. "You're going to fall. I've seen it over and over again—even among Christians, even among pastors. When we lose our humility, we're headed down a dangerous trail."

The life of the King and Warrior is for all men, Jerry believes, not just for those who display their courage on military battlefields, in sports venues, or in what some

"MEN ARE INSTINCTIVELY WARRIORS, AND WE NEED TO NURTURE AND USE IT IN THE RIGHT WAY."

their lives in Scripture and community with other men. He's seen and experienced firsthand the benefits of fighting battles—in the war zone and in everyday living—as a team.

"The Bible is very clear," he offers. "As iron sharpens iron, so one man sharpens another. We need fellowship with people of the same faith. It's through that fellowship we find encouragement in our own faith and are able to encourage others in theirs."

Jerry believes a man who grounds himself in God's Word and in community will be better equipped to react when life's bullets start flying. "Men are flawed and filled with all kinds of problems," he explains. "It comes down to what's in our hearts. If our hearts are filled with the desire to follow Christ and we're in constant communication with Him through prayer and the study of

would view as exciting or dangerous occupations. "Each of us is the same to God," he says. "The guy sitting in a cubicle is no less important to God than I am. God has a task for him—a mission for him. But the guy who takes the attitude, 'Well, my life's not exciting.' Make it exciting! Seek God's will for your life and He'll put you somewhere He wants you to be. We've got to recognize that all of this comes together for the good of God's Kingdom." 33

The **Four Faces** of **Manhood**
PART TWO: **LOVER / FRIEND**

SESSION **FIVE** | Training Guide **NOTES**

The **Four Faces** of **Manhood**
PART TWO: **LOVER / FRIEND**

I. INTRODUCTION

1. In the last session we unpacked two of the Four Faces of Manhood,[1] the King Face and the Warrior Face.

    *   The King Face creates order and provision. It provides direction. It leads with integrity. It allows us to be a **blessing** to those entrusted to our care.

    *   The Warrior Face shows our courageous energy and demands from us purposeful initiative. A man who wears the Warrior Face is a man of **action**.

2. In this session we'll look at the Lover Face and the Friend Face.

    *   These faces stretch our _____ capacity and can be unnatural for many men.

    *   Many men suffer from a stunted and reduced masculinity because they have never valued or learned to navigate their own **heart**, their own feelings, and their own emotions.

    *   Relational capacity requires men to engage _____.

    *   1 Thessalonians 2:7-9 – "Instead, we were like young children among you. Just as a nursing mother cares for her children, so we cared for you. Because we loved you so much, we were delighted to share with you not only the gospel of God but our lives as well. Surely you remember, brothers and sisters, our toil and hardship; we worked night and day in order not to be a burden to anyone while we preached the gospel of God to you."

    *   According to Stu Weber "whether on a football field, in a battle zone or under the roof of your own home, a man's willingness to show affection and care . . . to _____ . . . mark him as a leader and a man of God."[2]

---

[1] This session has been influenced by Stu Weber, "Four Pillars of a Man's Heart: Bringing Strength into Balance" (Multnomah, 1997). The Four Faces of Manhood are not necessarily intended to reflect only psychological categories, but rather are a point of reference to discuss the various roles, responsibilities, and relationships experienced by most men.
[2] Stu Weber, "The Heart of a Tender Warrior", 29.

II. **THE LOVER FACE** | SHOWING TENDER CARE

1. The Lover Face is primarily associated with tender care for others and a willingness to be emotionally **vulnerable**.

2. The Lover Face reflects _____ energy. It is characterized by tenderness, sensitivity, beneficial care, emotional openness, physical affection, and verbal communication. Lover Face in action:

   - Picks up on wife's real needs
   - Together time with wife
   - There for his family
   - Connects on a emotional level
   - Student of his kids
   - Says, "love you…" "proud of you…" "you're special…"

3. Examples of warriors who could also wear the Lover Face:

   - U.S. Army Major Sullivan Ballou[3]
   - King David

4. Caricatures of the Lover Face

   1) If a man's Lover Face is pushed too far, he can "show love" by becoming critical, harsh, and demanding of his wife and kids - _____ .

   2) A cold and withdrawn man - disconnected, detached, and **isolated**.

   3) If a man's Lover Face is pushed too far, he can also become over-dependent on women or relationships in general - _____ .

---

[3] The text of Sullivan's letter is taking from "Historical Document: Sullivan Ballou Letter," The Civil War, Public Broadcasting Service. Online: http://www.pbs.org/civilwar/war/ballou_letter.html.

III. **THE FRIEND FACE** | PURSUING CHARACTER-SHAPING FRIENDSHIPS

1. The Friend Face is primarily associated with a man's relational capacity to **connect** with other men.

2. The Friend Face reflects connecting energy. It is characterized by loyalty, accountability, encouragement, challenge, and fun.

3. We must learn to _____ genuine friendship with other men. Great friendship provides companions who can carry burdens and celebrate life's great moments with us.

4. You can't climb the mountain of manhood and reach its pinnacles if you are _____ from other men.

- Proverbs 17:17 "A friend loves at all times, and a brother is born for adversity." (ESV)

- Proverbs 27:17 "Iron sharpens iron, and one man sharpens another." (ESV)

- Biblical, soul-level friendships are priceless.

    ○ They require our **time**
    ○ They require us to be _____

5. Caricatures of the Friend Face:

- If a man's Friend Face is pushed too far, he can become dependent on those around him –
  The _____.

- If a man does not have enough of the Friend Face, then you get the typical, friendless,
  disconnected male - The **Loner**.

- Pursue _____ friendships.

IV. CONCLUSION

1. Wise is the man who can learn to wear these different faces of manhood.

2. Like everything we've said, you cannot fully embrace these Four Faces of Manhood unless
    you first embrace a right relationship with God and the provision He has made for us
    through Jesus Christ.

DISCUSSION / REFLECTION QUESTIONS

1. Did you identify more with the Lover Face or the Friend Face? Do you need to grow as a lover or as a friend?

2. Are you emotionally engaged at home? How could you encourage your wife or kids this week?

3. Discuss your capacity to connect with other men as good friends. Are you devoting the time needed to build soul-level friendships? Are you being others-centered?

SUPPORTING RESOURCES

Weber, Stu. *Four Pillars of a Man's Heart: Bringing Strength into Balance*. Multnomah, 1997.

The content in the supporting resource above does not necessarily reflect the opinion of Authentic Manhood. Readers should use recommended resources but form their own opinions.

Finding Compañeros By Jeff D. Lawrence

I *recently read Lonesome Dove,* Larry McMurtry's Pulitzer Prize winning novel made famous by the television miniseries many consider the greatest ever (starring Tommy Lee Jones and Robert Duvall). McMurtry's story follows a group of men on a cattle drive from Mexico to Montana. In many ways, the book is about men, their internal drives or passions, and the friendships they share along the way. This motley group assembled over time, but the core of the group served as Texas Rangers during the days when they fought real battles throughout the region. Through many eventful, often difficult, years together, the men had become "compañeros." These relationships weren't perfect, but they were characterized by intense loyalty, sacrifice, honesty, and memories. Every guy needs relationships like these, but few have them.

As I've observed guys who become real compañeros, I've discovered four things that create movement toward meaningful relationships: props, plans, risks and laughs.

GUYS NEED PROPS

Women seem to get together with other women and start talking deeply without effort, but guys aren't like that. You put them together and all you get is something along the lines of "how's work?" or "you playing fantasy football again this year?" Those two conversations can fill an entire evening.

In general, guys don't talk openly and freely without an external prop. It may be a task, a mission, a hobby, a shared history or some other event that brings them together. Men become close on a three-thousand mile cattle drive. They open up during a long winter in the trenches of wartime. They are brought together by an adventurous road trip. It isn't always something grand. It may be something as simple as a regular hunting trip, a golf foursome or mission trip. It may be group of friends from your college dorm or a church small group. There is not any "magic" prop, but there is almost always some kind of prop that brings the guys together initially.

My group of friends and I came together as friends during college, but those friendships expanded through a college road trip to bury a "time capsule" on the Texas-Mexico border (modeled loosely on the movie, "Fandango"). We each included something of great personal value and a list of spiritual commitments and life goals in the bottle. Ten years later, we returned to dig it up. That event become an annual long weekend together that has become a highlight in our lives.

If you want to find real friends, I suggest you grab a group of guys and initiate some unique activity. In male relationships, activity opens the door for conversation. Men start talking deeply after they've worn themselves out, made fun of one another or blown something up in a bonfire.

GUYS NEED PLANS

Past performance does not guarantee future success. Just because some prop brought you together for a unique time of relating as friends, you may not continue in that kind of friendship in the years ahead. Most guys who have not found life-long compañeros reflect on certain friendships with a nostalgic longing to go back, maybe even with a tinge of sadness. They are sweet memories, but they are just that: memories of something good that once was but is now gone. Friends rarely intend to lose touch with one another. *If your experiences together are going to grow into deep, lasting relationships, you need to commit to a plan.*

With my group, we decided to take an annual trip together. We pick a destination and a date, and we all fly in for a long weekend each year. My "Fandango" trip with this group of 6 men helps me hit my annual laugh quota in single weekend. This takes a real commitment, but it's worth everything it takes to make it happen. Our wives

sacrifice on the home front to allow us to go. We take time off work. We split the costs evenly to make it fair (sometimes, we pick up the tab for one another when finances are tight). This commitment propelled us from being college friends to becoming life-long friends.

The bottom line is that you won't become compañeros without regular time to laugh, play, and goof off together. This usually takes one person in the group who initiates an ongoing plan for being together and gets a commitment from the group. A plan creates a path for deepening relationships as you journey through the ups and downs of life together.

Most of the time, a particular place or activity becomes a big part of the group's identity. Guys seem to have a desire for a tradition that makes this time special. As men move from the free-wheeling college years to the responsibility of their 30's and 40's, they need time "away" from the normal routine of life. I'd encourage you to try something that allows for a break from your normal responsibilities and demands some real commitment from one another.

GUYS NEED RISKS

The third element I see is risk. If there is no risk, you will settle into a cycle of conversation that repeats itself over and over without taking you anywhere. Think about your relationships with your father or brother or co-workers for a minute. I bet you could write a script for most of those conversations as they revolve around the same topics with each phone call. This is just what guys do. We are strange beings. We privately long for a deeper relationship but we almost never acknowledge it.

Friends must continually take risks by sharing life at a vulnerable level. It amazes me how risky it feels to share what is happening in my heart even with my most trusted friends. We've been sharing life together for twenty years, but it still feels threatening to let them see my hurts, my unhealthy desires, my anger, my dreams, and my joys. It also brings freedom. The more I share, the more I'm freed up to be myself around them.

The bottom line is that you won't become compañeros without regular time to laugh, play, and goof off together.."

Most groups need a guy with the guts to be honest in front of others. Sometimes, it means saying, "You know what guys? I struggle with _____." Or, "You know what hacks me off about my life right now? It's _____." In our group, it seems to be a different guy who leads out each year with an honest and bold statement about his life. Each time someone opens the door to his heart, I think to myself, "OK, here we go." It's become my favorite part of our trip. I find out that I'm not that weird, or maybe that I'm just as weird as everyone else. Somehow, that's one of the things guys need to know: we are all jacked up. That kind of vulnerable sharing is relational fuel for men. Like a car, you have to refill the vulnerability tank regularly or the friendship runs out of gas.

GUYS NEED LAUGHS

With men, laughter both precedes and follows relational risks. *Guys need to laugh, and I've found that guys won't share openly until they have laughed freely.* If you want

guys to open up, you'd better crack one another up first. Some men don't know how to laugh. Because of this, people will rarely feel comfortable enough around them to be honest about what's in their hearts. Be careful sharing too much of yourself with men that can't laugh. The other side of this is that men who have shared openly laugh even harder. The trust and confidence gained in deep relationships lead to uncontrollable laughs that roll out until they bring tears.

For guys, friendship never happens as spontaneously as we'd like. It takes props, plans and risks, but the investment leads to a kind of laughter that is only shared by true compañeros. 33

Jeff D. Lawrence is a follower of Jesus, husband to Nan, and father to Mike, Luke, Jake, and Kate. Check out his blog at jeffdlawrence.com.

ROAD TRIP!

Nothing gets men focused like time away from the rigors of daily demands. With that in mind, here are recommendations for brief but memorable getaways and quality bonding time without breaking the bank:

1. **BARBECUE TOUR-** Make a three-day loop through Missouri, Tennessee, Alabama and the Carolinas for some of the best barbecue in America featuring a variety of styles. You might want to allow yourself an extra day off for recovery.

2. **FENWAY PARK-** Every man should make the pilgrimage to Major League Baseball's oldest active venue. If you time it right, you can enjoy watching the hometown Boston Red Sox battle their hated archrival, the New York Yankees.

3. **FLY FISHING-** Read up and seek the help of a guide if you're a beginner, then take off for a truly challenging fishing experience in one of the world's picturesque rivers. A refreshing way to unplug from the chaos of a busy life.

4. **HIKE THE APPALACHIAN TRAIL-** 2,181 miles of beauty extending from Maine to Georgia. If that's not enough, the International Appalachian Trail extends into Quebec, Canada. Watch out for black bears, rattlesnakes and moose!

5. **NASCAR-** Even if auto racing isn't your thing, it's an experience every man should have—feeling the thunder of a 40-car field coming down the straightaway under a green flag. Bring your earplugs and some sun block.

6. **NATHAN'S HOT DOG EATING CONTEST-** Held every July 4 for roughly 100 years, join 40,000 live spectators in Brooklyn to watch international rivals Joey Chestnut and Kobayashi attempt to break Chestnut's record 68 hot dogs in ten minutes.

7. **ROBERT TRENT JONES GOLF TRAIL-** Eleven gorgeous locations featuring 468 challenging holes of golf—all within a day's drive of one another in the state of Alabama. A great way to spend a three-day weekend.

8. **RANCH EXPERIENCE-** Horseback riding, river rafting, hunting, fishing and camping under the stars are just some of the experiences men can have at one of the hundreds of working ranches in North America.

9. **BARBER VINTAGE MOTORSPORTS MUSEUM-** The world's largest collection of motorcycles with more than 1,200 different models. Bikes on display range from 1902 to current-year, with styles ranging from recreational to racing. Located outside of Birmingham, Alabama

10. **CIGAR MASTERS IN BOSTON-** If you enjoy a good stogie, there's no better place to visit than Cigar Masters in Boston. Schedule a private rolling demonstration to see how a truly good cigar is made, then light up!

SAN DIEGO CHARGERS QUARTERBACK PHILIP RIVERS IS IN FULL WARRIOR MODE.

As 63,122 bloodthirsty Oakland Raiders fans in full throat attempt to break his unit's concentration, Philip scans the defense. Outside linebacker likely blitzing from the left end. Inside linebacker coming through the four hole. Time for a hot read.

A quick glance at the play clock shows nine seconds and counting.

Philip begins his cadence sending the left wideout in motion. The snap. A three-step drop. Tailback picks up the inside blitz. Philip fires to the right, a quick in route just as the outside linebacker launches his shoulder into the quarterback's ribcage and drives him to the ground. Philip looks up in time to see the tackle downfield. A gain of six. Success. A lineman helps Philip to his feet and the cycle begins again.

BY GRANT GUFFIN

QUARTERBACK PHILIP RIVERS ON FRIENDSHIP, FAMILY AND FOOTBALL

Just another day at the office for one of the NFL's top gunslingers, a passionate competitor who won't back down from anyone—be it a 250-pound linebacker bearing down like a locomotive or a lightning-fast defensive back in tight man coverage. He's even known to talk a little trash to get into an opponent's head. Anything to let his teammates know their leader is willing to lay it on the line *every* given Sunday.

This Warrior mentality has served him well. Combined with his natural gifts, strong work ethic and knowledge of the game, it's made him a selection to multiple Pro Bowls, the NFL Alumni's Quarterback of the Year, and ACC Athlete of the Year.

But to think of Philip Rivers as merely a skilled Warrior would be to miss out on much of what's also at the heart of the man—the face of the friend and lover.

THE FRIEND

Philip learned everything he knows about being a friend from one of *his* closest friends—his dad, Steve Rivers.

He recalls tagging along as a boy while his dad coached high school football at schools in north Alabama. Football was much more than simply his dad's profession—it was an all-consuming family affair for the Rivers, which, for eleven years, consisted of Steve, his wife Joan and son Philip (another son and a daughter would then be added to the mix).

Recreation time, dinner conversations, fall weekends, and interactions with people in the community often revolved around the sport; and while most kids would take the bus home from school, young Philip would get a lift to the high school so he could work as the team's ball boy, relishing time near his dad and the team environment.

Football felt natural, comfortable and fun to Philip because his parents made it that way for him. And from the beginning, father and son looked with anticipation to the days Philip would be part of one of Steve's teams. "He and I said it many times," Steve recalls, "'I can't wait 'til you're out there playing.' He wanted to play so bad."

When those years finally arrived, they didn't disappoint, though they passed far too quickly for all involved. "There's laughs, memories and things we talk about to

this day," Philip says. "I remember that last game, getting beat. He and I in the locker room—we were the only two in there—and just giving each other a big hug, because it was the end. It was something we'd looked forward to since I was a kid and now it was over." Even now, the memory causes both father and son to get misty-eyed.

"I think the one thing he always appreciated most was his players," Philip explains. "Players that maybe years later would come back and say what an impact he had on them. Or just the relationship and how he pushed *every* guy. Maybe someone who didn't play that much or wasn't very good, but he coached him like he was the *best guy on the team*. Seeing his passion for the guys is why I play with a little of that coach in me. I have that same passion and interest in each and every guy."

When the time arrived for Philip to embark on what would b as a college quarterback at Nor he left home with a clear unders meant to be a teammate and frie who'd call out the best in his te their successes and lift them up w going well. The kind of friendship h years by his dad.

"In the football world, what's r when your team wins, when you championship or a division, whe

success. When I'm 45 years old, the memories of football will be there and hopefully we'll have won some championships; but it'll be the locker room, the laughter on the bus and in the huddle, the weight room, the meeting room, and those relationships that'll hopefully mean the most."

THE LOVER

It wasn't often something took thirteen year-old Philip's mind off of sports. But he knew from the time he met her there was something special about Tiffany Goodwin.

He was an eighth grade athlete; she was a cute seventh grader with a sweet disposition. The more he knew about her, the more she captured his heart. Philip recalls seeing her at the ballpark one summer night and pointing her out to his mom: "'You see her over there? That's a good girl.' That was important to me: her values, her faith and who she was."

Unlike most young romances, theirs stood the test of time—through junior high, high school and his first year at North Carolina State. Then, finally growing weary of dating her, he decided it was time for a change. So he proposed.

TIFFANY AND I WANT TO SURROUND OURSELVES WITH A GROUP OF PEOPLE WHO CAN HELP THOSE KIDS FIND A MOM AND A DAD.

Philip and Tiffany Rivers were married in 2001. Fifteen months later he became one of the few sophomore quarterbacks in the nation leaving practice each day to go home to his wife and baby daughter. Philip had never been happier, and it showed on the field, as he led the Wolfpack to four consecutive bowl games, ultimately finishing his college career as Division I-A's second all-time leading passer with more than 13,484 yards.

In the years since, as both his football career and family blossomed (six kids, at last count), one thing has surely remained the same. "I spend as much time as anybody watching film and putting in the time," he explains, "but when it's over I want to be home with Tiffany and the kids. That's where I'm needed and that's where I want to be."

Adds Philip: "We like to be together. We're all together at night in the den or we all go back when everybody goes to bed. We like to be around one another. If we don't eat dinner together, our kids will let us hear about it. **You can tell when they know they're loved and cared for, what kind of impact that has on them.**"

"It's a passion there because I care about football, and it's a passion here because I care about (my family). You think you love somebody as much as you can when you get married, but it grows with every child you have. You have another child and you think, 'Well, my love's got to be spread out over all of these', but our marriage is only stronger."

The love doesn't ebb and flow with on-field performance: "Nothing is better than coming home—and it's a lot better after a win—but you come home after a loss and open the door and here they come running. 'Daddy's home!' They're about to knock you down. And you know, I didn't play very well, we just got beat, but they love me the same, and our family is what's most important."

His love for family doesn't end there. While participating in a calendar photo shoot with a San Diego-based adoption and foster care program, Philip was moved by the stories of some of the kids who were without permanent families. **Discussing the situation with Tiffany, they formulated the idea to launch Rivers of Hope, a foundation that seeks to support foster care and adoption efforts in San Diego County.**

"When you read it in the newspaper and it's a statistic, it's so easy to turn the page; but it's different when you actually see that it's real, that these kids are there and there are so many. We're right here and we feel like this is where we can help the most—and where I feel like I can give back and help this community the most is to help these kids in this town who watch me play on TV on Sundays that need me to help them. Tiffany and I want to surround ourselves with a group of people who can help those kids find a mom and a dad."

"The love we have for our kids and the way they need their mom, how I see them react to her, how the whole family structure goes—and how much different things mean to them, tucking them in at night and little things that mean a lot to them—you can take that for granted and think that happens in every household, but it doesn't. Until you dig and see real life cases and realize they're right here in our backyard, you realize you can't help them all; but I can help this one, and this one, and hopefully it grows from there." 33

Seasons

SESSION **SIX** | Training Guide **NOTES**

Seasons

I. INTRODUCTION

1. In the last two sessions we discussed the Four Faces of Manhood. Your manhood can't be just one dimensional, but needs be able to express itself appropriately given different situations.

2. Those on the path of Authentic Manhood are not only aware of different situations in their life, but they are also aware of the different _____ of life.

3. In this session, we'll look at the life stages of a man. What should life look like in your twenties? Or forties? Or seventies and beyond? We'll discover some helpful principles that can guide you through each stage of life and the unique battles you'll face along the way.

II. KEY IDEAS

1. _____ Engineering

    •   Begin with the **end** in mind

    •   _____ the lives of Godly men before us

2. The Power of_____

    •   Men who have already experienced the season we're in right now.

3. Anticipate **transition**

- Wise to _____ for the major transitions
- The Laws of the harvest

4. We reap what we sow

- We reap **more** than we sow
- We reap in a different **seasons** than we sow

III. **SPRING** | AGE 0 TO 20—IDENTITY

1. In this season a man comes to terms with his _____.

2. The key to this stage is transitioning to adulthood well.

3. The key questions of this stage:

- Who am I?
- Who am I not?

IV. SUMMER | AGE 20 TO 40—LEARNING AND GROWING

1. Potential Dangers of your 20's:

    •   Getting lost in extended _____ is not an option for
        Authentic Manhood

    •   Handling **sexual** energy:

        ○   "For this is the will of God, your sanctification: that you abstain from sexual immorality;
            that each one of you know how to control his own body in holiness and honor, not in the
            passion of lust like the Gentiles who do not know God." 1 Thessalonians 4:3–5 (ESV)

2. The major opportunity of your 20's:_____, _____, _____!

3. The key questions for your 20's:

    •   What do I want out of life?

    •   Where will I distinguish myself professionally?

    •   How am I different from my parents?

- What do I really believe?

- What skills do I need to develop?

- Around what person or conviction will I organize my life?

4. The major opportunity of your 30's: _____.

5. A key word to remember during your 30's: **margin**.

- Without margin, _____ are compromised

6. Key questions for your 30's:

- How do I _____ the demands made on my life?

- Have I allowed enough time for a spiritual life and authentic relationships?

V. **FALL** | AGE 40 TO 60—INFLUENCE

1. There can be a great _____ in this season.

2. Key questions for this stage:

   • Have I **achieved** everything I wanted?

   • Do I have dreams that are unfulfilled?

   • Can my mistakes be redeemed?

   • Are my **accomplishments** fulfilling?

3. The major danger of this season is a mid-life _____.

4. The great opportunity of this season can be summed up in one word: influence.

   • David Levinson calls men between the ages of 45 to 60 the "dominant generation." Levinson says that the guys in this season create and implement the governing ideas in every sector of society—whether it's politics, business, religion, art, or science.[1]

[a] David Levinson, "The Seasons of a Man's Life" (Ballintine Books, 1978), 29.

VI. **WINTER** | AGE 60 AND BEYOND—SAGE

1. Marked by _____, experience and respect.

2. The greatest danger of this season is for a man to buy the lie that he can no longer **contribute**.

3. The major opportunity of this season is to take advantage of your _____.

VII. **CONCLUSION**

1. Regardless of the season of life you are in, as men, we are all called to create and cultivate— not just for a particular season, but for our entire life.

2. We are called to follow the example of Jesus.

3. We are created to live a life of truth, passion, and purpose.

4. As men on a journey toward Authentic Manhood, we now know how to do that.

    • Reject passivity

    • Accept responsibility

    • Lead courageously

    • Invest eternally

DISCUSSION / REFLECTION QUESTIONS

1. How would you advise younger men who are about to enter your current or previous life stage?

2. How have you engaged older men in your life who can help guide you on life's journey?

3. This session discussed potential dangers for different seasons of life. What are the particular dangers you need to guard against in your current season?

SUPPORTING RESOURCES

Levinson, Daniel J. *The Seasons of a Man's Life.* Ballantine Books, 1978. Professor Daniel Levinson describes the male adult life cycle based on a 10-year study conducted at Yale.

MacDonald. Gordon. *A Resilient Life: You Can Move Ahead No Matter What.* Nelson Books. 2004. Author and retired pastor Gordon MacDonald writes about the "resilience" needed to face life's many challenges and stages.*

The content in the supporting resources above does not necessarily reflect the opinion of Authentic Manhood. Not all of the books are written from a Christian perspective. Readers should use recommended resources but form their own opinions.

ACTION PLAN

YOUR STRATEGIC MOVE | SESSION ONE : **MANHOOD REALITIES**

_____

_____

YOUR STRATEGIC MOVE | SESSION TWO : **CREATE AND CULTIVATE**

_____

_____

YOUR STRATEGIC MOVE | SESSION THREE : **MANHOOD DEFINITION**

_____

_____

YOUR STRATEGIC MOVE | SESSION FOUR : **FOUR FACES OF MANHOOD – PART 1 KING/WARRIOR**

_____

_____

YOUR STRATEGIC MOVE | SESSION FIVE : **FOUR FACES OF MANHOOD- PART 2 LOVER/FRIEND**

_____

_____

YOUR STRATEGIC MOVE | SESSION SIX : **SEASONS**

_____

_____

Outliving Your Life By Tierce Green

Singer-songwriter Billy Joel (multi-Grammy and American Music Award winner; Rock & Roll Hall of Fame) sang these lines to his hit song "My Life" back in 1978: "I don't care what you say anymore, this is my life. Go ahead with your own life and leave me alone!" It tells the story of an old friend (they "used to be real close") who got tired of the monotonous routine of his life; so he "closed the shop, sold the house" and "bought a ticket to the West Coast." Then, he did "a stand-up routine in LA."[1]

You at least have to give a guy credit for having the courage to march to the beat of a different drummer. Bucking the conventional standard can be a smart move but not when it means living out your life centered on yourself and shutting others out. That's not a dream worth following.

This is the conventional plan to live out your life: Go to school and get a good education; get a good job; work hard at your job and hope it will turn into a good career. Along the way, find a good wife, have some kids and raise a good family. If everything goes according to plan, you will have a good retirement that will allow you to live out your life in reasonable comfort. It's all good, right? (Oh, yeah ... and then you die.)

For most men, the payoff at the end feels less than satisfying. Along the way, a lot of guys feel restless and bored, suspecting that the process is flawed; but, they just keep their heads down and hope for the best. Underneath the surface, you can feel it. It's like a low-grade fever – you're not sick enough to stay in bed, but you're not well enough to really enjoy life either.

A common mantra among business gurus says, "Your system is perfectly designed to give you the results you're getting." What's true in business is true in life. If the system of how you live out your life is only producing a nice collection of stuff with no eternal significance, then you need a new system.

Audi's "Truth in Engineering" tagline is a powerful promise ... and it's just talking about metal and rubber! *The truth in the way men are engineered – the truth in the way we are designed by our Creator – is that we are built to live for something greater than ourselves. We are wired to outlive our life.*

Outliving your life might sound too epic and unattainable, but a few minor adjustments can make all the difference. Let's say you board a ship in San Diego on your way to Honolulu. If the navigation coordinates are just a few degrees off, you could miss Honolulu and wind up in Tokyo. A slight course correction in whatever season of life you are in can change your trajectory and guide you to a more fulfilling destination.

Here are three course-correcting adjustments for outliving your life:

1 DISCOVER A TRANSCENDENT CAUSE.

What are you living for that is bigger than yourself? Having a transcendent cause means you leave more than a carbon footprint. It is the opposite of marking time and just living out your life. It is unconventional.

A transcendent cause is really a paradox, because living for something greater than yourself is one of the greatest things you can do for yourself. Teaching his children to be "others centered" and "outward focused" is one of the biggest things a man can do to outlive his life. It is the gift that keeps on giving.

2 LEVERAGE YOUR INFLUENCE NOW.

Some men on the front end of their careers, or those who feel stuck in the middle, give in to the idea that they don't really have an influence yet. While the fall and winter of a man's life are typically the seasons of his greatest influence, any man

[1] Billy Joel, "52nd Street" (Columbia, 1978). | [2] John C. Maxwell, "The 360° Leader" (Thomas Nelson, 2005), Section I. | [3] "The greatest among you will be your servant." (Matthew 23:11, NIV) | [4] "... If anyone wants to be first, he must be the very last, and the servant of all." (Mark 9:35, NIV) | [5] 33:The Series, The Seasons of a Man's Life "(Authentic Manhood, Fellowship Associates, 2011). | [6] "The kingdom of heaven is like treasure hidden in a field. When a man found it, he hid it again, and then in his joy went and sold all he had and bought that field." (Matthew 13:44, NIV)

in any season of life needs to realize his potential to impact others right where he is.

John Maxwell exposes the myths of leading from the middle in his book *The 360° Leader: Developing Your Influence from Anywhere in the Organization*. Maxwell says that some people believe leadership comes simply from having a position or title. So they wait, thinking, "When I get to the top, then I'll learn to lead." They believe they can't really make a difference unless they are on the top.[2]

The truth in our engineering is that most things are accomplished because of relationships and reputation, not because of position. According to Jesus, the man who is truly great is the one who serves others.[3] Jesus said if a man wants to be first, he must put himself last.[4] Look around at the relationships and responsibilities you have been given. Outliving your life by serving and influencing others starts right now.

3 INVEST FOR ETERNITY.

A man who invests eternally wants to make a difference now, but he also sees into the future. He understands the Laws of the Harvest. The first law is we reap what we sow. The second is we reap more than we sow. The third is we reap in a different season than we sow.[5] *When a man begins to leverage his influence and invest in others, teaching them how to live for something greater than themselves, it could begin a culture shift for the next generation and make an eternal difference.*

Jesus Christ, our model for Authentic Manhood, challenges all men to be part of something He calls the "Kingdom of God" or the "Kingdom of Heaven." He urges us to understand its value and to forsake everything else to possess it, to acknowledge that it is the only thing worth living for.[6]

Countless things compete for our attention. I was reading a magazine that targets men and tells us what we need to be healthier and happier and came across an ad that leaped off the two-page spread. Written above the hood of a shiny new silver Chevy Camaro was this: "You could live without it. If you call that living." Can you feel that? I want a test drive right now!

Hold your horsepower, and think about this. You could live without a transcendent cause, without really influencing others for eternity. You could keep your head down on the conveyor belt of conventional manhood, work hard and carve out a pretty good life – all for you. You could just live out your life that way. If you call that living. 33

NEVER TOO EARLY, NEVER TOO LATE.

Seasonal Trivia by the Numbers

AGE: ACCOMPLISHMENT:

6 Christopher Beale becomes the world's youngest published male author.

19 Igor Sikorsky designs and builds his first helicopter.

23 George Armstrong Custer named Brigadier General in the U.S. Army.

28 Cartoonist Charles Schulz premieres "Peanuts" comic strip in newspapers.

36 Mohandas Gandhi implements a strategy of non-violent protest in India.

44 Sam Walton launches Wal-Mart.

45 George Foreman becomes boxing's oldest heavyweight titleholder.

53 Theodor Geisel (Dr. Seuss) pens "The Cat in the Hat."

64 Oscar Swahn wins Olympic gold in shooting; at age 72 he finishes fourth.

65 Harland Sanders (a/k/a Colonel Sanders) franchises Kentucky Fried Chicken.

75 Nelson Mandela elected President of South Africa.

77 Astronaut John Glenn returns to space aboard the space shuttle Discovery.

80 George Burns becomes the oldest male Oscar winner in a competitive category.

95 Jack LaLanne releases a book on health and fitness.

100 Fauja Singh runs the Toronto Waterfront Marathon in 8:11:06.

THE EVOLUTION

of

RANDY SINGER

BY GRANT GUFFIN

RANDY SINGER WAS IN A GOOD FRAME OF MIND AS HE STEPPED ON THE TREADMILL.

Sure, he was in a doctor's office for his biennial heart check-up, but Randy was healthy as a horse—the doctor said so himself. And if he could stay on the treadmill one second longer than on his last visit, he'd avoid having a scope run down his throat in favor of another, non-invasive test.

Following twenty-three minutes of grueling treadmill time, Randy cooled off while basking in his anticipated reward, an EBT scan to detect the build-up of calcium in coronary arteries.

LIFE WAS EXCEPTIONAL *for* RANDY.

Now in the fall season of life, he'd already experienced more career success than most men enjoy in a lifetime. His marriage of twenty years to Rhonda was thriving; his kids were the kind of children every parent hoped to have.

Then his doctor—normally an upbeat, jovial type—entered the room with a serious look on his face. Randy's score on the EBT scan should have been somewhere in the teens or twenties. Instead, it was closer to six hundred. Randy was diagnosed with a condition causing massive calcification of the coronary arteries—meaning he was at high risk for a fatal heart attack.

> **"IT WAS A SLAP IN THE FACE, A REMINDER OF MY FRAGILE MORTALITY AT A TIME I HAD BEEN PLANNING ON LIVING ANOTHER 40 YEARS."**

"It was a slap in the face," Randy explains. "A reminder of my fragile mortality at a time I had been planning on living another 40 years. And I always thought when somebody tells you that—you have a very serious heart condition—I always thought it would make me frantic, that I'd want to spend my remaining time on earth doing as much as I could, making sure I invest every second wisely because there's not as many seconds as I thought there were."

SPRING | SHAPING AN IDENTITY

A hard charger from the start, Randy dreamed of someday attending law school at Cornell, then embarking on a noble career as a "Warrior for justice".

Randy took a brief detour from the dream, becoming a history teacher and basketball coach at a small boarding school in upstate New York. Randy enjoyed the experience—building, motivating and encouraging kids.

But the dream continued to call out to him. So, after five years of seasoning, Randy enrolled in William and Mary School of Law. Three years later, he graduated second in his class and accepted a job with a prominent local firm. The dream was becoming a reality. He would become a "Warrior for justice" after all.

SUMMER | HEALTHY MARGINS VS. CAREER ADVANCEMENT

Randy quickly rose through the ranks, establishing himself as one of Virginia's top trial attorneys, successfully handling cases at the state and federal levels. In time, he was named head of the trial division at his firm, and was lead counsel on several high profile cases.

The dedicated practice of law came naturally to Randy. Establishing margins with his time didn't. He often yielded to his competitive drive and continued working at times he could've—and should've—been more involved at home. In time, Randy realized his priorities were out of balance.

"In the early years, your kids are willing to come into your pattern," Randy explains. "As they get older, they develop their own patterns of life. I realized I needed to come into their world, find out what their dreams are, figure out how best to engage them."

"I didn't spend enough time with my kids when they were young," Randy laments. But God was good to Randy, giving him the opportunity to learn from, and correct, past mistakes. "He gave me years in my kids' high school days to be the dad I should be."

Randy made the necessary adjustments to be present—mentally and physically—at home. In turn, his family made an adjustment in their thought process that freed Randy to do the work he needed to do with a clear conscience.

"Rhonda and the kids needed to know they were the priority. If our families have our attention for the things that matter most to them, they won't begrudge us doing what we need to do at our work."

Another adjustment came in the form of sound advice from a mentor: "He told me that giving my family events and experiences was more valuable than giving them things."

Randy recalls a particularly meaningful adventure with his son. "We took a trip to a ranch for a father-and-son deal. There was a high ropes course, cliff diving, belly flops into the lake. It really flipped the father-son thing. He was leading me physically. And it was so cool, allowing him to be the leader in the family."

FALL | EXERTING INFLUENCE

"I was at an event in 1995 or '96 where the speaker referenced Cortes (16th century explorer). He told his men to burn the ships; we're not going back. The speaker at the event asked, 'What's so important in your life you're not willing to burn the ships for Christ?'"

"I realized the practice of law had become an idol in my life. Sometimes God gives us a dream, but the dream—not God—becomes our all-consuming passion. Then God takes it away from us. Sometimes we have to allow a dream to die to be sure we're using it for God's glory and not for ourselves."

> "THE CALL OF GOD ON OUR LIVES IS IRREVOCABLE, AND WE CAN'T LET OBSTACLES OR FAILURE HOLD US BACK."

Randy left the practice of law and invested his expertise in roles with a national organization and a television network.

In 2007, God returned the dream—no longer an idol—to Randy. He launched his own practice, the Singer Legal Group, specializing in civil litigation and business and ministry consulting. He also accepted a role as Attorney in Residence at a local law school and helped launch a church.

Randy also pursued another passion—writing. Now, with more than a dozen books to his credit, Randy has established himself as a prolific fiction author—a milestone he'd never have reached if he'd allowed initial rejections to derail him. "The call of God on our lives is irrevocable," he observes, "and we can't let obstacles or failure hold us back."

WINTER | POURING INTO OTHERS

The frightening heart diagnosis had indeed been a wake-up call—a startling reminder to Randy of his own mortality. But it didn't make him frantic, as he'd imagined.

Instead, given time to process this new challenge in his life, Randy experienced something completely unexpected—peace. "I realized it wasn't about impact; it was about faithfulness. I might just be the pawn on the chessboard, so I'm pouring my life into people where God has called me. If I'm faithful in that I can quit worrying about my legacy. God has the master plan—He'll take care of that."

Randy has made frequent return visits to the doctor's office in the years since his initial diagnosis.

His doctors are pleased at how his heart condition has plateaued—some arteries even naturally creating their own bypass system to circumvent those that are calcified.

Randy continues to write, practice law, work with his church, and be the husband, father and friend God has called him to be. He has become content and even excited about the sphere of influence God has given him—and he's embraced it with all his heart. "In recent years I've been more about community," he says. "My office is a mile from my home, my church is only a couple of miles from that. There are local people I'm pouring my life into, and that's where I'm supposed to be for this time."

Looking back through the early seasons of life, he believes there are lessons he can pass on to those who follow: He encourages the man in the spring season of life to "get in the line for servants. There are lots of men who want to jump in the line to be leaders, but the line for servants is short. Be a servant to your family."

As he anticipates the transition to the winter season of life, Randy is inspired by the example of his father who—at age 58—performed some of his most significant life work. "So many men have decided if they can just survive until they die they'll have done what God called them to do," Randy offers. "That's prevent defense—playing not to lose. God may have so much more for you. It's never too late. I still have mountains to climb." 33

it's
NEVER
TOO
LATE.

A Man and His Design- Answer Key

SESSION ONE: MANHOOD REALITIES

I.   Men
1. Confusion
3. Pain
5. Drifting
7. Problems
8. Vision

SESSION TWO: CREATE AND CULTIVATE

I.   1. Wake-up
2. Clarity

II.   1. Leadership
- Creates
- Cultivates

2. Him
3. Create and Cultivate
4. Social and Spiritual
5. Chaos
6. Natural born

III.   1. Failed
2.   1) Fruit
- Will

2) Fig leaves
- Cover, Perform

IV.   1. Cared
2. Jesus
3. Enables
4. Sinners
5. Offense
7. Power

V.   1. Childish
- Cheap thrills
- Life-giving

2. Cowards, Critics
- Don't
- Criticize

3. Understanding

VI.   1.
- Trust
- Wired
- Model

SESSION THREE: MANHOOD DEFINITION

I.   1. Led
2. Self-effort

II.   1. Will
2. Work
3. Woman

III.   1. Jesus
- Righteousness
- Fulfilled

3. Conventional
4. Authentic

IV.   1. Passivity
2. Responsibility
3. Courageously
4. Invest

V.   2. Life-giving

SESSION FOUR: FOUR FACES OF MANHOOD – PART 1 KING/WARRIOR

I.   1. Expands
2. One- dimensional
3. Multi-dimensional
4. King, Warrior

II.   1. Righteous
2. Integrity
3.
- David

4. Leadership
5.
- Tyrant
- Compromiser